THAT ALL MAY BE ONE

That All May Be One

PERCEPTIONS AND MODELS OF ECUMENICITY

Harding Meyer

Translated by

William G. Rusch

WILLIAM B. EERDMANS PUBLISHING COMPANY
GRAND RAPIDS, MICHIGAN / CAMBRIDGE, U.K.

255 Jefferson Ave. S.E., Grand Rapids, Michigan 49503 /
P.O. Box 163, Cambridge CB3 9PU U.K.
Translated by William G. Rusch from the German
Ökumenische Zielvorstellungen by Harding Meyer
(Göttingen: Vandenhoeck & Ruprecht, 1996
[Bensheimer Hefte; H. 78: Ökumenische Studienhefte 4]).

Printed in the United States of America

05 04 03 02 01 00 99   7 6 5 4 3 2 1

Library of Congress Cataloging-in-Publication Data

Meyer, Harding.
[Ökumenische Zielvorstellungen. English]
That all may be one: perceptions and models of ecumenicity /
Harding Meyer; translated by William G. Rusch.
p.   cm.
Includes bibliographical references.
ISBN 0-8028-4348-4 (pbk.: alk. paper)
1. Ecumenical movement.   I. Title.
BX8.2.M4913   1999
280′.042 — dc21   98-53603
CIP

The English edition of this book is dedicated in appreciation and with fond memories to the following institutions in the United States of America, which have honored me with the bestowal of a doctorate (h.c.):

Luther College, Decorah, Iowa, 1988 — D.D.

Lenoir-Rhyne College, Hickory, North Carolina, 1993 — Litt.D.

Trinity Lutheran Seminary, Columbus, Ohio, 1994 — D.D.

Contents

Note

For guidance concerning the abbreviations used in this work, the reader should consult:

Theologische Realenzyklopädie, Abkürzungsverzeichnis, 2nd ed., ed. Siegfried M. Schwertner (Berlin and New York: Walter de Gruyter, 1994).

Additional resources are:

A Documentary History of the Faith and Order Movement: 1927–1963, ed. Lukas Vischer (St. Louis: The Bethany Press, 1963); trans. from *Die Einheit der Kirche, Material der Ökumenischen Bewegung,* Theologische Bücherei, Vol. 30 (Munich, 1965).

Documentary History of Faith and Order: 1963-1993, ed. Günther Gassmann (Geneva: WCC Publications, 1993; Faith and Order Paper 159).

Growth in Agreement: Reports and Agreed Statements of Ecumenical Conversations on a World Level, ed. Harding Meyer and Lukas Vischer (New York/Ramsey: Paulist Press and Geneva: World Council of Churches, 1984); trans. from *Dokumente wachsender Übereinstimmung, Sämtliche Berichte und Konsenstexte interkonfessionaler Gespräche auf Weltebene,* Vol. 1, 1931–1982 (Paderborn: Verlag Bonifatius-Druckerei and Frankfurt am Main: Verlag Otto Lembeck, 1983).

Note

The Ecumenical Movement: An Anthology of Key Texts and Voices, ed. Michael Kinnamon and Brian E. Cope (Grand Rapids: William B. Eerdmans Publishing Co. and Geneva: WCC Publications, 1997).

Preface to the English Edition

Two factors are obvious in the contemporary religious scene: first, the history of the church in this century will be marked indelibly by the ecumenical movement; second, as this century draws to a close the ecumenical movement is itself marked by a crisis. Although ecumenical literature abounds to the degree that no one person can comprehend its totality, surprisingly little has been written, certainly in English, to address the question of the continuity, integrity, and indivisibility of the ecumenical movement. How this question is resolved within the ecumenical movement, and within the churches, will say much about the ecumenical movement and its future. I realize, of course, that this distinction is false, but to raise it is to indicate something of the present ecumenical dilemma.

It is because this question is so pressing and not merely a theoretical discussion that this volume by Harding Meyer is such a valuable contribution. Here is an impressive description of the multifaceted ecumenical movement, of its relation to a variety of concepts of the church and its unity, and of the several models of union and their relation to recent accents on mission and ethical concerns. Anyone wishing to understand the modern ecumenical context and how it arose will profit from this account, now available in English for the first time.

I have endeavored to have the author speak in present-day English and at the same time to be faithful to his German. Whenever possible, I sought to give the bibliographical references in English so that these resources will be accessible to the English-speaking reader.

It is a task that I have enjoyed: to make available a dear friend to a wider readership. How well I have performed this work others must judge. In the process I must thank the author for his assistance, although any mistakes that are found in the English text are mine.

A word of gratitude must also be expressed to William B. Eerdmans, Jr., and Norman A. Hjelm. Without the support of both this edition would not have been possible.

William G. Rusch
Reformation, 1997

1. *The Question of Perceptions of Ecumenicity*

1.1. The Necessity and Difficulty of the Question

The desire for unity among Christians and churches never results in actual, concrete steps toward overcoming divisions without at least an implicit notion of the kind of unity or community toward which one is striving in the first place.

This is valid for the ecumenical movement as a whole. This movement, as it engaged Christendom at the beginning of our century, is not only a sign of general ecumenical concern and desire. It is also the comprehensive historical expression of a purposeful struggle for the visible unity or fellowship of Christians and churches.

A goal-oriented movement of this sort must articulate as clearly as possible the aims commonly agreed upon by its adherents. Both clarity and common agreement of the definition of aim are indispensable. For diffuse concepts of the aim deprive the ecumenical movement of its orientation and paralyze its dynamics. Divergent concepts of the aim endanger its cohesion, its inner unity and indivisibility, and would bring the movement into self-contradiction.

Therefore, from the very beginning the question of the perceptions of ecumenicity has accompanied the ecumenical movement as one of its central concerns. From the very beginning this question has also disclosed its complexity.

Three factors in particular make the question a complex one:

First: The ecumenical movement is not, and never was, a unified and homogenous phenomenon. Diverse motivations sustain the ecumenical movement. They find expression in differing ways of seeking unity, in differing "movements," all of which together constitute "the" ecumenical movement. This diversity of motivations and movements is reflected in differently shaped perceptions of ecumenicity.

For this reason, it was and is necessary to discover and preserve the right interrelation of these movements that are determined by different motivations and perceptions.

Second: The struggle for unity or community is decisively influenced by the understanding of church and of ecclesiastical unity that Christians and churches bring with them from their particular tradition. The differences in the understanding of church rooted in tradition have a direct bearing on the determination of the ecumenical aim.

Thus, the question was and is how the aim of ecumenicity can be determined in a manner that both takes account of existing ecclesiological differences and still has sufficient power to provide a point of orientation for the *common* ecumenical struggle.

Third: Like all of the life and action of Christians and churches, the ecumenical movement is embedded in the multiform and changing context of human history. Of course, this historical context cannot fix the aim of the ecumenical movement. Nonetheless, the perception of this aim is conditioned by the historical milieu. And for this reason, the perception itself is part of the multiformity of and the change in the historical context.

Furthermore, the ecumenical movement and its agents have their own history. New ecumenical developments and insights cause the ecumenical aim to appear with new and different perspectives and in a new and different light.

Thus perceptions of ecumenicity are variable and preliminary. Their historical changeability and tentativeness notwithstanding, the necessity of clear and common perceptions of ecumenicity, as well as the search for them, must be continuously upheld and maintained.[1]

1. Even if the sought-after unity is understood as "community" in the sense of "mutuality relationship" and "relatedness of what is different," there is no reason to consider the search for such community as lacking the nature of an "intentional, aim-oriented process." See Konrad Raiser, *Ökumene im Übergang: Paradigmenwechsel in der ökumenischen Bewegung* (Munich: Chr. Kaiser, 1989), 127. This text is not contained in the English translation of the Raiser book. See footnote 133 in chapter two.

1.2. The Formulation of the Question

In order to answer the question of ecumenical aims, one must make a twofold distinction.

a. The "Aim" and "Perception of the Aim"

The *aim* of the ecumenical movement is the community of all who believe in Christ, the "unity of Christians." Provided that all who believe in Christ belong to his church — the "community of the faithful" — it can just as well be said that the aim of the ecumenical movement is the "unity of the church." Yet because this church of Jesus Christ exists historically in special ecclesial bodies, that is, communities that are local, regional, or marked by particular traditions, one can also say that the aim of the ecumenical movement is the "unity of the churches."

All three expressions mean the same and are therefore interchangeable. They are the elementary declaration of the aim of the ecumenical movement in each of its forms.

This elementary declaration, however, immediately calls for precision and interpretation. It demands *perceptions* of this aim and cannot continue without them. It is this theme that is the subject of this volume.

As closely related as aim and perception of the aim indeed are, their distinction is by no means artificial and thus pointless. To say that "unity of Christians," "unity of the church," or "unity of the churches" is the goal of the ecumenical movement is paramount to stating the basic and comprehensive aim. But there is a need, indeed, for more precise "perceptions" or definitions of this goal. At the same time, however, these perceptions must remain within that framework of the basic aim, if they are to be perceptions of ecumenicity.

The distinction between aim and perceptions of the aim in a certain sense thus keeps the latter in check. It takes care that in their diversity and changeability the perceptions of the aim do not evade the specificity and distinctiveness of the ecumenical movement. For the ecumenical movement is not just any humanitarian, social, or political movement of unity, which can or should be taken up by

Christians and churches. Rather, according to its being, it is a movement of unity that arises from the Christian faith, is supported by Christians and churches, and is related to them in its aim.

This has nothing to do with Christian-ecclesiastical self-centeredness and constriction of the ecumenical movement. Such is determined not on the level of the elementary declaration of the ecumenical aim but rather on that of the perceptions of the aim. A Christian-ecclesiastical constriction of ecumenical effort occurs only when being a Christian and being a church are mistaken as ends in themselves, and Christian-ecclesiastical effort for unity is pursued in the shadow of this misunderstanding. On the contrary, when Christians and churches know that in what they are and do they are put into service by their Lord for his work of reconciling human beings to God and to themselves, they will also "perceive" and seek to realize the "aim" of unity in the light of this task. Thus one may certainly say that more is always at stake in the ecumenical movement than "the unity of the churches" — as the title of a Lutheran study document indicates[2] — but it cannot be said that the ecumenical movement is about something other than the church's unity.

b. "Understanding of the Unity of the Church" and "Models of Union"

In relation to the question concerning the "perception" or "perceptions" of the ecumenical aim, another distinction is required for the sake of clarity. This second distinction is, all in all, more familiar than the first but has prevailed only in recent times. It is of considerable importance, as will be shown below (cf. 3.1).

At its meeting in Louvain (1971) the Commission on Faith and Order of the World Council of Churches (WCC) once again raised the question of the perception of the ecumenical aim.[3] The reasons for this — on the one hand, a clear stagnation of negotiations for church union in different countries, on the other hand, the emer-

2. "More than Unity of the Churches. Study Document for the Fifth Assembly of the Lutheran World Federation," in *LR* 1 (1970): 43ff.

3. World Council of Churches. Commission on Faith and Order, *Faith and Order, Louvain 1971: Study Reports and Documents.* Faith and Order Paper 59 (Geneva: World Council of Churches, 1971), 230ff. (Cited in the following as Louvain.)

gence and prompt acceptance of bilateral ecumenical dialogue — will be discussed later. It is important to note first of all and in this context that the Commission functioned with a differentiation that was novel in its clarity: the distinction between "concepts of unity" and "models of union."

In relation to its subject matter, the distinction is clear. The "concepts of unity" are said to concern the fundamental understanding of "the nature of (the church's) unity": its essential characteristics and marks, its constitutive elements, and its basic requirements. The "models of union" concern the "forms of manifestation" of ecclesiastical unity, the details of its concrete assumption of form, of its form of materialization.[4]

Both are naturally closely tied together. The question of the models of union presupposes the question of the concepts of unity and its resolution. Yet this connection is not so close that each concept of unity contains its own model of union within itself. Rather, one and the same understanding or concept of unity can be realized in different models of union. An agreement in the understanding or concept of unity thus in no way implies that an agreement also exists or must exist in regard to the model of union, that is, about the form in which unity is to be realized. The differentiation is thus not only sensible but also necessary.

After the Faith and Order meeting in Salamanca (1973) and the immediate preliminary work relating to that meeting, the terminology remained largely constant. There is reference to "concepts of unity and models of union" which had been the title of the study document (1972). Therefore, it seems obvious to follow this terminology. Since the discussion has repeatedly shown, however, that the two terms — "concept" and "model" — easily become blurred "understanding of unity" will replace "concept" in the following discussion. "Understanding of unity" corresponds more closely to the issue at hand and differentiates itself more clearly from "models of union."

"Understanding (or 'understandings') *of the unity of the church"* and *"models of union"* will, therefore, be the two leading terms in the following discussion.

4. Louvain, 236.

2. *Understanding of the Unity of the Church*

Coming from their own ecclesiastical traditions, Christians and churches introduce into the ecumenical movement their own and, for the most part, specifically characterized understanding of the unity of the church. Thus, something akin to a confrontation of different understandings of unity occurs in the ecumenical movement.

It is important, however, to see that this confrontation of different understandings of unity takes place *within* the ecumenical movement. This means that the difference of the understandings of unity does not go so deep as to prevent the commonality of ecumenical effort. Their difference notwithstanding, all understandings of unity lead rather into the ecumenical movement and the common effort for the unity of the church.

This situation points to fundamental commonalities, which, before and beyond all their difference, bind together the different understandings of unity and, at the same time, are fundamental for the ecumenical movement as a whole.

It is, above all, three such commonalities that are now to be designated in the form of three guiding principles.

2.1.1. Unity Belongs to the Nature of the Church
(The Basic Ecumenical Conviction)

The credo of the early church confesses "one, holy, catholic, and apostolic church" (the Nicene Creed). It adheres to that to which the New Testament bears witness. The church is a community of all who through faith and baptism are "in Christ." The uniqueness of Christ constitutes, at the same time, the unity of those who are in him. The metaphor of the church as "body" or as the "body of Christ" clearly expresses this. Just as a body cannot be sundered so also the "body of Christ," the church, cannot be sundered. The metaphor of Christ as the "head" of the body strengthens this further. Other images in the New Testament of the church also speak of it in this manner, so that it becomes clear that from its very being, from its basis, the church is the *one* church. It is one church as "people" of the one God, as "bride" of the one Lord, as "temple" of the one Spirit. Each of these images resists being turned into the plural. The Letter to the Ephesians summarizes all this. The unity of the church grows from the unity of that which constitutes the foundation of the church, the one Spirit, the one Lord, the one faith, the one baptism, and the one God and Father (Eph. 4:1-5). Therefore, even where the New Testament speaks of the church in the plural, that is to say, of the individual congregations, it is clearly referring to the one church of God that in different locations (such as Corinth or Rome) manifests and concretizes itself.[1]

In brief, the New Testament does not speak of the church without, at the same time, speaking of its unity.

Thus the unity of the church is a matter of Christian faith and confession and not something subject to our disposition or a matter of considerations of mere utility.

The different views of the unity of the church as they meet in the ecumenical movement have their common starting and reference point in this conviction of the "essential unity" of the church. This conviction is nothing less than the basic conviction that sustains the ecumenical movement.

This basic ecumenical conviction implies two further convictions.

1. Cf. the Pauline expression *"hē ekklēsia hē ousa en . . ."* (1 Cor. 1:2; 2 Cor 1:1; in addition, see *ThWNT,* vol. 3, 508 [German ed.]).

2.1.2. The Essential Unity of the Church Is Presupposed in Every Effort for Unity

(The Ecumenical Indicative)

"God . . . assembles . . . for himself an eternal church on earth" declares a hymn of the church.[2] In its conciseness this phrase falls short of no theological formulation. It refers once more to what was stated previously: it is God who assembles the one church. It is not the faithful but God who is the subject when we speak of the church as "the assembly of all the faithful." This is strengthened through the reference to the idea that the church belongs to God. God creates the one church not as he creates the world or the things of the world. He creates it as belonging to himself, as "people of God," "body of Christ," "temple" of the Holy Spirit. Therefore, the church in its unity is indestructible, "eternal," as the hymn declares. It is not preserved through the strength or endangered through the weakness of human desire for community. Its indestructibility is based on its belonging to God, and therein lies the promise that the church will remain "his church" — and thus in its God-given unity — irrespective of the whole power of evil (Matt. 16:18).

This also belongs to the Christian faith and confession. The credo of the early church recorded it by fixing in the confession the phrase "the one, holy, catholic, and apostolic church." For only what God is himself and has done irreversibly can be the object of faith and confession.

Here soteriology and ecclesiology, the understanding of salvation and of church, mesh together. Like the salvation of human beings, so also is the church a deed and a gift of God. Both are characterized by the indicative, by the "once and for all" (cf. Heb. 7:27; 9:12; 10:10), and both are antecedent to all human action.

All ecumenical "activity" also presupposes this indicative of the present, obtaining unity of the church. Because such activity neither creates nor establishes the unity of the church, all ecumenical "declarations of unity" that describe the ecumenical aim thus first of all affirm this very indicative: The unity of the church is a "God-given" unity; it is God's "gift," his "present."

The essential and always given unity of the church may be seen

2. *Evangelisches Gesangbuch,* Hymn 245.

more strongly in its Christological or in its trinitarian aspects, that is, as rooted in the one Lord and head of the church, or as rooted in the unity of the Father, the Son, and the Holy Spirit. The Christological foundation prevailed in the first decades of the ecumenical movement.[3] Subsequently, it was enlarged on a trinitarian foundation which is still true today.[4]

2.1.3. The Essential Unity of the Church Must Be Lived and Be Made Visible
(The Ecumenical Imperative)

What then is the task of the ecumenical movement? And what is the aim of the ecumenical effort?

Its aim is to let the given unity become "visible."

"Visible unity" — for a good number of years now, this has been a firm and very important comprehensive description of the aim by which the ecumenical movement and ecumenical activity are oriented.

Since 1975, the World Council of Churches lists as its first "function and purpose" in its constitution the following:

> To call the churches to the goal of *visible unity* in one faith and in one eucharistic fellowship expressed in worship and in common life in Christ, and to advance towards that unity, in order that the world may believe.

3. Especially at the World Conference for Faith and Order in Lund (1952) ("Message, Final Report II, par. 11," in World Council of Churches. Commission on Faith and Order, *Faith and Order; the Report of the Third World Conference at Lund, Sweden, August 15-28, 1952* [London: SCM, 1952]; in the following cited as Lund) and at the Assembly of the World Council in Evanston (1954) in the report of its section 1: "Our Oneness in Christ and Our Disunity as Churches," in World Council of Churches. Assembly (2nd: 1954: Evanston, Ill.), *The Evanston Report, the Second Assembly of the World Council of Churches, 1954* (London: SCM, 1955), 82–83 (in the following cited as Evanston). Cf. the Assembly of the World Council in Amsterdam (1948), 51. (References to assemblies of the World Council of Churches and world conferences of Faith and Order are to the official reports, unless otherwise noted.)

4. This is clear especially since the Assembly of the World Council in New Delhi (1961). World Council of Churches. Assembly (3rd: 1961: New Delhi, India), *The New Delhi Report: The Third Assembly of the World Council of Churches, 1961* (London: SCM, 1961), 116 and 118–19 (in the following cited as New Delhi).

This corresponds almost verbatim to the present constitution of the Commission on Faith and Order (Paragraph 2), except that it refers first to the indicative of the unity given in Christ and only then formulates the imperative:

> The aim of the Commission is to proclaim the unity of the church of Jesus Christ and to call the churches to the *goal of visible unity* in one faith and one eucharistic community which is expressed in worship and in the common life in Christ, so that the world may believe.

The predicate of "visibility" did not always appear as such in the description of the aim of ecumenicity, the unity of the church, and did not have the status that it is accorded in recent times. It certainly did appear time and again in older documents of the ecumenical movement.[5] But the idea of "visibility" was expressed alternately as follows: that "the one life of the one body should be made manifest before the world,"[6] that the task was "to give expression to the oneness of the church of Jesus Christ,"[7] to give "expression [to it] in life and work,"[8] to "bring it into the light of day,"[9] "truly to represent it,"[10] or "to cause it to appear outwardly."[11] These terminological

5. World Conference on Faith and Order (2nd: 1937: Edinburgh, Scotland), *The Second World Conference on Faith and Order, Held at Edinburgh, August 3-18, 1937* (Edinburgh: Lothian, 1937), 231–32 (in the following cited as Edinburgh) and in Lund (1952), 16 and 37; New Delhi, 117–18; Toronto Declaration of the World Council of Churches (1950) (see Michael Kinnamon and Brian E. Cope, eds., *The Ecumenical Movement: An Anthology of Key Texts and Voices* (Grand Rapids: Eerdmans, 1997), 465–68.

6. World Conference on Faith and Order (1st: 1927: Lausanne, Switzerland), *Reports on the World Conference on Faith and Order, Lausanne, Switzerland August 3 to 21, 1977* (Boston: The Secretariat, 1928), 464–65 (in the following cited as Lausanne).

7. Earlier Constitution of Faith and Order.

8. Toronto Declaration of the World Council of Churches (1950); see Kinnamon and Cope, eds., *The Ecumenical Movement,* 463.

9. Evanston, 84.

10. Evanston, 85.

11. World Conference on Faith and Order in Montreal (1963); World Council of Churches. Commission on Faith and Order. Theological Commission on Christ and the Church, *Final Report of the Theological Commission on Christ and the Church* (Geneva: World Council of Churches, Commission on Faith and Order, 1963), 39.

variations, however, are of no substantive importance. The predicate "visible" can certainly be replaced by other predicates — provided that the meaning and function of the concept of "visible unity" is preserved.

Two important aspects are above all at issue here.

First, the concept of "visible unity" — as a designation of the unity sought — seeks to preserve the distinction between God's action as a gift and the human action of response also in the sphere of efforts for Christian unity. In light of this, the predicate "visible" initially serves in general to make a conceptual distinction between the unity sought and that already given. This makes clear on the conceptual level as well that it cannot be the aim of the ecumenical movement to create the unity of the church as if the Christian confession in the one church were invalid or as if it waited for humans to render it true through their actions.

Second, the concept of visible unity seeks to characterize the unity sought by us in a basic respect. The predicate "visible" now has the specific function to declare: The unity of the church, which we believe in and confess as God's gift, is not a unity separate from the visible, empirical reality of our Christian life and action. Just as little as the church is a *"civitas platonica"* is its unity a *"unitas platonica."* It wishes rather to take on form in the visible, empirical reality of our life and action. In this respect — and only in this respect — does the unity of the church become a unity *assigned* to us and the aim of ecumenical endeavor.

Thus the language of the "visible unity" corresponds to what is generally true for Christian existence. The new life, which we have received in faith, seeks to find expression in the renewal of our lifestyle. The indicative pushes toward the imperative, "If we live in the Spirit, let us also walk in the Spirit" (Gal. 5:25). The promise of salvation leads to exhortations, and the exhortations point to the concrete, visible formation of our life and action.

In the same sense, the unity that is a gift to us also becomes a unity that is a task for us. The ecumenical indicative gives rise to the ecumenical imperative. The word from the Letter to the Galatians can thus be turned into an ecumenical one: If we are one, then let us live and act in unity. Indeed, the Pauline admonitions for unity among Christians and in the congregations derive always from the indicative of their oneness and call upon them to allow this given oneness in their life and action to be a visible reality (1 Cor. 12:4ff.; Eph. 4:3-6).

2.1.4. Reservations and Specifications Concerning the Language of the "Visible Unity" Sought

Basic, shared ecumenical convictions do, indeed, include the notion that the aim of ecumenical activity is to actualize the given unity of the church in the concrete, visible reality of Christian life and action. Nevertheless, the language of the "visible unity" sought often encounters reservations. Some of these reservations can be addressed; with others the ecumenical movement will have to live.

a. The recurring fear that the concept of "visible unity" defines the aim of ecumenicity from the start in the sense of a comprehensive, unified church organization proves to be unfounded and invalid in view of the above. This will be demonstrated fully later in this volume.

b. A more detailed answer, by contrast, is called for by the question of whether the concept of "visible unity" implies that the essential unity of the church, which we believe and confess, is a completely "invisible unity" and that, therefore, it must still be "made visible" in every aspect. This question is related, of course, to the more inclusive problem of the "visibility" and "invisibility" of the church that has also been discussed since the Reformation in polemical theology. It can be said that, on the whole, the answer to that question in the ecumenical movement is clear and fits into the comprehensive ecclesiological discussion about the visibility and invisibility of the church.

The relevant documents of the ecumenical movement never say that the unity of the church, in which we believe and which we confess as an always given unity, is "invisible" according to its being or that its visibility must first still be conferred. Neither can discussion of the "spiritual unity" as the foundation of "visible unity" be understood this way.[12] Similarly, these documents never profess the belief that the unity of the church is, or would be, rendered completely "invisible" through ecclesial divisions. Against this

12. E.g., Edinburgh, 231–32.

stands the assurance that there are clearly visible foundational aspects of ecclesial life that are present in all churches in spite of divisions, in particular the explicit and public confession in the Triune God and Christ, the Lord and Redeemer, the Holy Scripture, the sacraments of baptism and the Lord's Supper, an office of Word and sacraments.[13]

Hence the conclusion follows that the unity given by God to the church is obscured[14] and distorted[15] in its visibility by the ecclesiastical divisions. The ecumenical problem and the starting point of ecumenical effort lie not in an invisible unity, but rather in a visibility of unity that is concealed, obscured, and distorted by ecclesial divisions. The effort for visible unity can therefore be understood also as "growth."[16] It is a question of the unity becoming "more completely visible."[17]

This clarification is important also for the concrete effort for "visible unity." That effort does not begin from the division of the churches, at point zero, as it were. Rather, there is already a "partially realized oneness of the church,"[18] a "certain fellowship"[19] of the separated churches. There are always concrete, visible starting points for this effort.

c. In the ecumenical movement, and even in the World Council of Churches, there are churches that, given their understanding of church, continue to have reservations about the notion of "visible unity" as determining the aim of ecumenicity. We shall discuss this later. On the one hand are the churches that "view church exclusively as a universal, spiritual communion." For them "visible unity is unnecessary or even undesirable" because "the church is by nature invisible."[20] At the other end of the spectrum are churches, such as

13. Cf. Evanston, 86–87, and also the Decree on Ecumenism of the Second Vatican Council (*Unitatis Redintegratio,* 3; abbreviated as *UR* in the following).

14. Lund, 27.

15. Evanston, 84.

16. Evanston, 84.

17. New Delhi, 118.

18. Evanston, 84–86.

19. *UR,* 3.

20. Thus reports the Toronto Declaration of the World Council of Churches (1950); see Kinnamon and Cope, eds., *The Ecumenical Movement,* 465, on the conceptions of individual member churches of the World Council of Churches.

the Orthodox churches or the Roman Catholic Church, who are convinced that the one church has already found its visible realization in them and, for that reason, prefer to speak of the sought after unity as "reuniting."

Different as these two reservations are, they are apparently not serious enough to have prevented the member churches of the WCC that uphold them from embracing the constitution of the WCC and its call for "visible unity"[21] or from using the notion of "visible unity" to define the purpose of their dialogue with other churches. These are reservations, therefore, with which the ecumenical movement must — and obviously can — live.

Thus we reach the point where the influence of the different understandings of specific confessions about the church and its unity become perceptible.

2.2. Traditional and Specifically Confessional Forms of the Understanding of Unity

What now are the specific forms of understanding the unity of the church as they are brought into the ecumenical movement by the different ecclesiastical traditions? It will become apparent how the particular understanding of unity corresponds to the unity that is lived in the particular church or confession.

In the following, five such, for the most part, confessionally specific, "understandings of unity" will be identified and described. Our guiding question will be, What constitutes the unity of the church? Or stated otherwise, What are — from the viewpoint of this particular understanding of unity — the basic presuppositions that must be fulfilled if the churches are to live and act in visible unity?

21. The Constitution of the World Council of Churches III/1 (see 1.1.). In spite of what the Toronto Declaration refers to as the "ecclesiological neutrality" of the World Council of Churches, it also states that it "is simply a Christian duty of each church to do its utmost so that the church in its unity becomes visible." See Kinnamon and Cope, eds., *The Ecumenical Movement,* 466.

2.2.1. Churches of the Reformation

Because the Reformational struggles of the sixteenth century associated concern for the truth of the gospel with that for the unity of the church, those churches that emerged from the Reformation — thus especially the Lutheran and Reformed churches — are able to key their own ecumenical endeavors to basic assertions about the unity of the church deriving from their origins. From the perspective of the history of theology, these Reformation assertions are, in fact, the first doctrinal statements on the church and its unity. On the Lutheran side, Article 7 of the Augsburg Confession of 1530 comes to mind and on the Reformed side especially Article 17 of the "Confessio Helvetica Posterior" of 1566.

Augsburg Confession, 7:

> It is also taught, that one holy Christian church must always be and remain, which is the assembly of all believers, among whom the gospel is purely preached and the holy sacraments are administered according to the gospel. For it is sufficient for the true unity of the Christian church, that the gospel harmoniously is preached and the sacraments administered according to the Word of God (Latin text: Et adveram unitatem ecclesiae satis est consentire de doctrina evangelii et de administratione sacramentorum). And it is not necessary for the true unity of the church, that everywhere the same ceremonies established by human beings be observed, as Paul says to the Ephesians (chapter) 4: "One body and one Spirit as you are called to one hope of your calling: one Lord, one faith, one baptism."[22]

Second Helvetic Confession, 17:

> Furthermore, we diligently teach that care is to be taken wherein the truth and unity of the Church chiefly *(potissimum)* lies, lest we rashly provoke and foster schisms in the Church. Unity consists not in outward rites and ceremonies *(ritibus externis),* but rather in the truth and unity of the catholic faith *(fides catholica).* This catholic faith *(fides catholica)* is not given to us by human laws, but by the Holy Scriptures, of which the Apostles' Creed is a compendium. And

22. From *BSLK,* 64, which includes the original Latin and German texts. Cf. Theodore G. Tappert, ed., *The Book of Concord* (Philadelphia: Fortress Press, 1959), 32.

therefore we read in the ancient writers that there was a manifold diversity of rites *(ritus),* but that they were free, and no one ever thought that the unity of the Church was thereby dissolved. So we teach that the true harmony *(concordia)* of the Church consists in doctrines *(in dogmatibus)* and in the true and harmonious preaching of the Gospel of Christ and in rites that have been expressly *(diserte)* delivered by the Lord.[23]

Here two aspects are especially prominent.

Communion in the Proclamation of the Gospel

First, *togetherness in faith,* the true ("apostolic") Christian ("catholic") faith, is placed at the center with great emphasis. In contrast to this, all else recedes in importance for the church's unity. In terms of the unity question, the personal faith of individuals is not so much at issue as is the church's proclamation of the faith, that is, the public proclamation of the gospel through Word and sacrament (baptism and the Lord's Supper), which awakens and strengthens personal and justifying faith.

This ecclesiastical, public proclamation of the faith can neither be left to the individual preacher, nor is it an event of proclamation that happens all by itself. If communion in the true Christian faith and with it the unity of the church are to be preserved, then a common theological ascertainment about faith in its content is required, one that gives the proclamation of the gospel a binding orientation.

Thus there is need for agreement in the proclamation of the faith: of the *"consentire de doctrina evangelii,"* as the Latin version of the Augsburg Confession renders "(preaching the gospel) harmoniously in pure understanding," or as the Second Helvetic Confession says, the *"concors praedicatio evangelii."* This agreement can be expressed and must be stated and formulated if it is to inform proclamation in a binding manner. Thus it has a "doctrinal" character. This already becomes clear terminologically in that in the Second Helvetic Confession *"in dogmatibus"* and *"in praedicatione"* go to-

23. The English translation is found in Arthur C. Cochrane, ed., *Reformed Confessions of the 16th Century* (Philadelphia: Westminster Press, 1966), 267–68. The original Latin is given in *BSKORK,* 252f.

gether, and in the Augsburg Confession the Latin *"doctrina evangelii"* stands for "preaching the gospel." The doctrinal character of the agreement in faith also becomes clear in that both statements are in the context of a doctrinal confession of the church, one which describes this agreement in faith, article by article, in terms of consensus statements.

Indeed, during the Reformation period and beyond, the struggle of the Reformation churches for the unity of the church concentrates itself ultimately on the struggle for consensus in doctrine.

Freedom in Ecclesiastical Customs and Traditions

Freedom in the area of ecclesiastical "ceremonies" and "rites" corresponds to this concentration on communion in the proclamation of the gospel (proclamation of faith). Here there is no need for uniformity; indeed, even the demand for uniformity is repudiated.

Still we must be conscious that a particular note is sounded in this for the Reformation.

What was understood as "ceremonies" and "rites" at that time was quite varied, ranging from the ringing of bells to regulations on fasting, from particular forms of worship and of the life of piety all the way to canon law and certain expressions of ecclesiastical office. These ceremonies and rites all share a common characteristic, however, in that they were not given to the church from the beginning by God and thus established in Scripture, but rather that they arose in the history of the church and are the result of ecclesiastical ordinances or decisions. This makes them in the view of the Reformation fundamentally "ceremonies instituted by human beings" (*CA* 7).

It is exactly for this reason that the unity of the church is not to be made dependent on the uniformity of ecclesiastical ceremonies or rites. For this would mean that the church and its unity are made dependent on human factors and would contradict the Reformation doctrine of justification and with it the gospel.[24] What is necessary in the strict sense for the unity of the church is only that which

24. This is shown clearly in the Apology of the Augsburg Confession, where the statement of Article 7 of the Augsburg Confession is explained. (See *BSLK*, especially 241–44).

makes the church church: the action of God in the proclamation of the gospel through Word and sacrament.

This in no way denies that those ecclesiastical ceremonies and rites, practices and institutions have the potential to be good and useful for the church and its unity. Thus there is a readiness, especially in the area of the Lutheran tradition, to preserve communion in these matters — provided that they serve the gospel and its proclamation. What is rejected is the demand that, for the sake of the unity of the church, unanimity is absolutely indispensable in these matters.

As regards what is actually necessary for unity, the distinctive feature of the Reformational understanding of unity is concentration on the agreement in the preaching of the gospel and in the administration of the sacraments. The clearly expressed agreement in the proclamation of the gospel is the decisive factor for visible communion with other churches. Yet the lack of such agreement with other churches has not led the Reformation to conclude that other churches are not proclaiming the gospel in Word and sacrament and therefore are not churches.

Communion in the Ecclesiastical Office (Ministry)

In view of this concentration on agreement in the proclamation of the gospel as a necessary condition for unity, the question arose again and again whether in the Reformation perspective ecclesiastical office and communion in ministry were of no import for the church and its unity.

The answer to this question is determined by the Reformation understanding of the gospel and ecclesiastical office. Since the gospel is always a proclaimed gospel and the sacraments are always distributed sacraments, is the office which proclaims the gospel and administers the sacraments "included," so to speak, in the preaching of the gospel and the administration of the sacraments? Just like the preaching of the gospel and the administration of the sacraments, the office is "no . . . human arrangement *(non . . . hominum est ordinatio),*"[25] but rather "an institution of God *(institutio Dei)*"[26] and

25. Second Helvetic Confession, 18.
26. Second Helvetic Confession, 18; Augsburg Confession, 5.

as such — not in its particular historical forms — belongs to the church. Precisely because the office is "included" in the gospel proclamation and the administration of the sacraments, it does not always need to be articulated explicitly in affirmations concerning the church and its unity. This indicates as well that the office, as a "service" *(ministerium)* to the proclamation of the gospel in Word and sacrament, is not on the same level with but rather is a subsidiary of and subordinated to the proclamation of the gospel. With regards to the church's unity, communion in ecclesiastical office cannot be given up, but the question of that communion is secondary to agreement and communion in the proclamation of the gospel in Word and sacrament and is answered from there in every decisive aspect.

To what extent this understanding of unity, which is rooted in their origin, has determined the ecumenical effort of the Reformation churches in the past and still determines it today cannot be clearly stated. The different assessment of the binding character of historic confessions of the Lutheran and Reformed churches is surely one reason why the ecumenical effort of the Lutheran churches on the whole follows the path of the Reformation understanding of unity more closely than do the Reformed churches.

2.2.2. Anglican Churches

The Anglican "Thirty-nine Articles" (Articles of Religion) of 1563 and 1571, which came into being in close connection to the Continental, especially the Lutheran, Reformation, also contain certain fundamental statements about the church and its unity. They are found in Articles 19 and 34.

Article 19:

> The visible Church of Christ is a congregation of faithful men, in the which the pure Word of God is preached, and the Sacraments be duly ministered according to Christ's ordinance in all those things that of necessity are requisite to the same. . . .

Article 34:

> It is not necessary that Traditions and Ceremonies be in all places one, or utterly like; for at all times they have been divers, and may

be changed according to the diversities of countries, times, and men's manners, so that nothing be ordained against God's Word.[27]

The "Chicago-Lambeth Quadrilateral"

These statements are, however, not as determinative for the Anglican understanding of the unity of the church as similar statements in the Reformation churches on the Continent. The Anglican understanding of unity is explained rather in a considerably more recent document, commonly referred to as the Chicago-Lambeth Quadrilateral. This was outlined by the North American theologian W. R. Huntington in 1870, accepted in the "House of Bishops" of the Protestant Episcopal Church in Chicago in 1886, and soon thereafter adopted by the Lambeth Conference in a slightly modified form. It has been repeatedly confirmed on the Anglican side and influenced the "Appeal to All Christian People" of the Lambeth Conference of 1920, one of the great calls to the unity of the church at the beginnings of the ecumenical movement.

Chicago-Lambeth Quadrilateral:

> That, in the opinion of this Conference, the following articles supply a basis on which approach may be by God's blessing made towards Home Reunion:
>
> a) The holy Scriptures of the Old and New Testament as "containing all things necessary to salvation," as being the rule and ultimate standard of faith.
>
> b) The Apostles' Creed as the Baptismal Symbol; and the Nicene Creed, as the sufficient statement of the Christian faith.
>
> c) The two sacraments ordained by Christ Himself — Baptism and the Supper of the Lord — ministered with unfailing use of Christ's words of institution, and of the elements ordained by Him.
>
> d) The Historic Episcopate, locally adapted in the methods of its administration to the varying needs of the nations and peoples called of God into the Unity of His Church.[28]

27. Book of Common Prayer, Articles of Religion, 19 and 34.

28. *The Book of Common Prayer,* Historical Documents of the Church, Lambeth Conference of 1888, Resolution 11.

This document thus offers what amounts to an ecumenical program by articulating from the Anglican perspective the constitutive elements of ecclesiastical unity. Even today it informs the ecumenical effort of the Anglican churches.

Two things are striking here: first, the emphasis on the Holy Scripture and its authority, and second, the significance for the community of believers ascribed to the symbols of the early church. Declaring the Apostles' and Nicene Creeds to be "a sufficient statement of the Christian faith" indicates that for the Anglican churches the struggle for a theological consensus that goes beyond that statement, developing and at the same time verifying this common faith, does not have the same elevated ecumenical significance as it does for the Reformation churches. It expresses similarly how the significance of a doctrinal consensus such as the "Thirty-nine Articles," in the sense that it fosters community, has increasingly receded in the historic development of these churches, especially in the favor of the common liturgy and the common episcopal order. This holds true also in relation to the communion of Anglican churches among themselves.

The Significance of the Office of Bishop

The Chicago-Lambeth Quadrilateral points as well to the obvious difference between the Anglican understanding of unity and that of the Reformation churches. It consists in the fact that the ecclesiastical office (ministry) is included not only implicitly but expressly, specifically in the form of the "historic office of bishop" — in essence, in the form of the office of bishop that goes back to the apostles and stands in continuous historical succession.

This stress on the historic episcopate is in good measure the fruit of inner-Anglican developments. The Church of England had preserved from the beginning the threefold office of bishop, priest, and deacon and took care that it be continued.[29] That did not mean, however, that foreign churches which had not preserved the episcopate, for instance in France and Germany, were therefore not held to

29. Cf. the Preface to the Ordinal of the *Book of Common Prayer* (1662) and what it says about the ordination of bishop, priest, and deacon.

be churches. Thus communion was possible with them even in the ministerial office. After the end of the Puritan Revolution and political take-over (1644–1660), the Restoration brought an increasingly higher evaluation of the episcopal structure of the church and of episcopal succession. This is reflected, for example, in the decision of 1662 that only those who had been ordained by a bishop were permitted to exercise an office in the Church of England.[30] This excluded communion in the office of ministry and hence *full* fellowship with nonepiscopal churches from then on. The Oxford Movement of the first half of the nineteenth century stressed the historic episcopate even more strongly. For this movement the episcopate in apostolic succession became a basis and criterion for being a true church and, as a result, a basic presupposition for ecclesiastical unity in the full sense.

This inner-Anglican development explains the fourth point of the Chicago-Lambeth Quadrilateral. Ever since, the question of communion in the historic episcopate has played a central role for Anglicans in their union negotiations and dialogues with Reformation and other Protestant churches, just as the question of Roman Catholic recognition of ordinations performed by Anglican bishops has figured prominently in the dialogue with the Roman Catholic Church.

2.2.3. Free Churches

In 1977, the Unions of Baptist Congregations in Austria and Switzerland and the largely Baptist Union of Evangelical-Free Churches in Germany drew up a "Confession of Faith," recommending it for use in their congregations. One of its sections is entitled "The One Body of Christ and the Separated Churches." It states the following:

> The Christian experiences the communion of the community above all in the local assembly of the faithful. In it baptism for the confes-

30. The Preface to the Ordinal (1662) states: "No persons are allowed to exercise the offices of bishop, priest, or deacon in this Church unless they are so ordained, or have already received such ordination with the laying on of hands by bishops who are themselves duly qualified to confer Holy Orders." This is still valid, even if the formulation of the Preface varies.

sion of faith is performed, and the one bread, bestowed by the one Lord, is broken and shared. That is why the local parish understands itself as the manifestation of the one body of Christ, filled with the one Spirit and fulfilled with the one hope.

The one Spirit bestows many gifts that not only in the local parishes but also in the churches separated from one another can result in mutually enriching diversity. Jesus Christ builds his community in different churches and communions. Still, in spite of differences and in spite of error and guilt on all sides, it cannot be the will of God that confessional barriers prevent the visible fellowship of all believers and thus their credible witness before the whole world. Therefore, we pray with the churches of the entire earth for renewal of all communities and churches, so that more mutual recognition becomes possible, and God leads us to the unity that he wants. Today it is not just the task of individual Christians from different churches, but rather a task of these churches themselves to take possible steps away from division and toward one another, to dismantle existing prejudices, to formulate and present objections conscientiously, to learn from one another, to pray for one another, and to glorify the common Christ in witness and service.[31]

If this text is understood on the larger horizon of free-church thought, one can recognize at least four special accentuations of the understanding of unity that are characteristic of the "free churches," that is, those churches that are derived from the Anabaptist movement of the Reformation or who understand themselves related to this movement and were strongly marked by the Revival Movements of the last three centuries.

1. The *personal faith* of every Christian, that is, that person's "acceptance of the grace of God"[32] and "mature decision for Jesus Christ,"[33] is extremely important as a fundamental feature of the free-church understanding of church. Everyone — regardless of church membership or denominational affiliation — who has experienced the grace of God and has been led by the Holy Spirit to conversion, who has in personal faith chosen Christ as Lord and been

31. Bund Evangelisch-Freikirchlicher Gemeinden in Deutschland, ed., *Rechenschaft vom Glauben,* II, No. 7 (1977).

32. *Rechenschaft vom Glauben,* I, No. 2.

33. *Rechenschaft vom Glauben,* II, No. 3.

guided by the Spirit into the way of discipleship, belongs to the church and forms together the one body of Christ. Only God knows them all, and, in this sense, the universal church, exceeding space and time, is "invisible."

As a result, the free church understanding of the church places from the start an especially strong and consistent accent on the *spiritual and free nature of the church* and its unity. The church is not connected in its essence to any kind of external and visible conditions and signs. These are subordinate to the personal faith that makes human beings members of the body of Christ. The believer's baptism of the Baptists is merely an especially clear expression of this aspect. And this faith, on the basis of which human beings unite with one another in the assembly of the faithful, is the "personal," "mature," and, in this sense, "free" decision of each person for Jesus Christ.

2. This strong stress on the spiritual nature of the church certainly does not mean that the church and its unity lack visibility. Unity of the church — "the communion of the congregation" — as the aforementioned text puts it, is concretely "experienced." To be sure, it is experienced and visible "above all in the *local assembly of believers*" — on "the level of local ecumenism," as one could say. In the local congregation as the free-will assembly of believers, the church is visible in its unity.[34] This local assembly of believers is not just one but is rather "the manifestation of the one body of Christ"

34. John Smyth, the founder of the first Baptist parish in Amsterdam (1609), speaks of the church as "visible church," and he is referring to the "visible church" when he views the church as constituted by "three things": "1. The true matter which are the payntes only. 2. The true form which is the uniting of them together in the covenant. 3. The true propertie which is communion in all holy things, & the powre of the Lord Jesus Christ, for the maintaining of that communion." See "Differences of the Churches of the Separation, 1608," in *Sourcebook for Baptist Heritage,* ed. H. Leon McBeth (Nashville: Broadman Press, 1990), 14f. In the first Baptist Confession of Faith (1644, art. 23) it is similarly stated: "The Church, as it is visible to us, is a company of visible Saints, called and separated from the world by the word and spirit of God, to the visible profession of faith of the Gospel, being baptized into that faith and joined to the Lord, and each other, by mutual agreement, in the practical enjoyment of the Ordinances, commanded by Christ their head and king." Cited by William R. Estep, "A Response to Baptism, Eucharist and Ministry: Faith and Order Paper No. 111," in *Faith, Life and Witness. The Papers of the Study and Research Division of the Baptist World Alliance 1986–1990,* edited by William H. Brackney (Birmingham, Ala.: Samford University, 1990), 4.

par excellence. Therefore, each local congregation possesses independence and autonomy. It itself "orders its life and its service."[35]

Here one finds a second, specific aspect of the free-church understanding of the church and its unity. The local congregations are certainly joined to one another: "through the one Lord and the one Spirit," through the communion in faith, through intercession and mutual help.[36] Associations beyond the local congregation, however — and for free churches these exist right up to the global level — are not churches in the proper sense but rather "unions" that do not impair the independence of local congregations as the actual manifestation of the church. Once again it is shown here how strongly the understanding of the church and its unity includes the element of freedom and with it the tension between the two — unity and freedom.

3. This freedom also determines the local assembly of believers as such in their unity and in their common life. The thought and practice of the *priesthood of all believers* perhaps finds its strongest expression in the free churches. "The common priesthood of all believers is the basic structure given to the Christian congregations by the Lord."[37] There is no fundamental "over-againstness" of office and community and, in this sense, no structure of office (ministry). All believers are given gifts by the Holy Spirit that serve the building up of the community and its common life: "There is no ungifted member in the body of Christ."[38] There are, indeed, "special services" and, in this sense, "offices" to which the congregation, recognizing the gifts of the Spirit, "calls" suitable men and women. Gifts of the Spirit and offices (ministries), however, serve the assembly and mission of the community of Jesus Christ "in the same manner."[39]

In this strong stress and concrete application of the notion of the priesthood of all believers lies a further characteristic of free-church understanding of the church and the unity of the church.

4. "Christ builds his community in different churches and communions," as the quoted text states. Therefore, it is contrary to

35. *Rechenschaft vom Glauben,* II, No. 5.
36. *Rechenschaft vom Glauben,* II, No. 5.
37. *Rechenschaft vom Glauben,* II, No. 5.
38. *Rechenschaft vom Glauben,* II, No. 5.
39. *Rechenschaft vom Glauben,* II, No. 5.

the will of God if "confessional barriers prevent the visible fellowship of all believers." For that reason, the free churches declare their belief in the ecumenical movement and participate in it as churches.

Of course — and this too is a characteristic of the free-church understanding of unity and efforts for unity — the affirmation of the ecumenical movement is often connected to *reservations vis-à-vis the concept and the aim of the "visible unity"* of the church. Free churches do not simply reject this goal, but rather they interpret and pursue it in light of their specific convictions regarding the church and church unity. The "visible unity" sought must not conceal the spiritual nature of the church and its unity and curtail the freedom of believers and their local assembly. Efforts to achieve unity that are oriented toward common church order and structures and toward theological consensus in faith fade in importance. As the quoted text states, it is ultimately a question of "renewal of all communities and churches" that leads to "more mutual recognition" among the churches. The aim of ecumenical endeavors is the free togetherness and mutuality of churches and Christians recognizing one another's intent to "glorify Christ together in witness and service."[40]

2.2.4. The Orthodox Church

The Orthodox understanding of church unity is not easy to grasp if one seeks to document it. Statements that are binding on or are received by all the Orthodox churches — comparable to those of the Reformation or Anglican churches or the Roman Catholic Church — do not exist. This is in accord with the fact that there is an established Orthodox "church consciousness" but no hard and fast Orthodox teaching about the church. Until now, one essentially could only refer to what official Orthodox delegations to assemblies or conferences of the World Council of Churches described — very often in the form of a special declaration — as the Orthodox understanding of the unity of the

40. Cf. also E. Geldbach, "Baptists and the Ecumenical Movement. A Strategy Paper," in *Faith, Life and Witness* (see footnote 34 above), esp. 43–46, "How Could Baptists Define the Goal of the Ecumenical Movement?"

church.[41] The Orthodox declarations to the Assembly of the World Council of Churches in Evanston (1954)[42] and New Delhi (1961) are important here. The following is an extract from the last of these.

> . . . For the Orthodox the basic ecumenical problem is that of schism. . . . The unity has been broken and must be recovered. The Orthodox Church is not a confession, one of many, one among many. . . . The Orthodox Church is aware and conscious of the identity of her inner structure and teaching with the Apostolic message (kerygma) and the tradition of the ancient undivided Church. She finds herself in an unbroken and continuous succession of sacramental ministry, sacramental life and faith. Indeed, for the Orthodox the apostolic succession of episcopacy and sacramental priesthood is an essential and constitutive and therefore obligatory element of the Church's very existence. The Orthodox Church, by her inner conviction and consciousness, has a special and exceptional position in the divided Christendom, as the bearer of, and witness to, the tradition of the ancient, undivided Church, from which all existing denominations stem, by the way of reduction and separation. . . . The common ground, or rather the common ground of existing denominations, can be found, and must be found, in the past, in their common history, in that common ancient and apostolic tradition, from which all of them derive their existence. This kind of ecumenical endeavor can be properly denoted as "ecumenism in time." Orthodox theologians suggest this new method of ecumenical inquiry, and this new criterion of ecumenical evaluation as a kingly rock, with the hope that unity may be recovered by the divided denominations by their return to their common past. By this way divergent denominations may meet each other on the unity of the common tradition.[43]

More recently, the Third Panorthodox Pre-Conciliar Conference in Chambésy (Switzerland, 1986) has made statements about

41. A collection of Orthodox documents and declarations on the ecumenical movement and the unity of the church is found in C. G. Patelos, ed., *The Orthodox Church in the Ecumenical Movement* (Geneva: World Council of Churches, 1978), and N. Thon, *Quellenbuch zur Geschichte der Orthodoxen Kirche* (Trier: Paulinus-Verlag, 1983), esp. 475–548.

42. Patelos, ed., *The Orthodox Church,* 94–96.

43. Patelos, ed., *The Orthodox Church,* 97f.

the Orthodox understanding of the unity of the church that are far more representative than the declarations of Orthodox ecumenical delegations.[44] These statements can be reproduced here only in part:

> 1. The Orthodox Church in its deep conviction and in its ecclesiastical consciousness to be the preserver and witness of the faith and tradition of the one, holy, catholic, and apostolic Church, firmly believes she occupies a central place in what concerns progress toward the unity of Christians.
>
> 2. The Orthodox Church realizes that too numerous and important departures from the tradition of the undivided church have occurred in the course of history for different reasons and in different ways. Thus in the Christian world views that differ from one another about the unity and real nature of the Church have been revealed.
>
> The Orthodox Church sees the unity of the church grounded in its foundation by our Lord Jesus Christ and in the communion of the Holy Trinity and in the sacraments. This unity is expressed through the apostolic succession and the patristic tradition and has been lived up to the present day within the Orthodox Church. The Orthodox Church has the commission and the duty to deliver the entire truth which is contained in the Holy Scripture and in the holy Tradition, and which bestows on the church its universal character. The responsibility of the Orthodox Church and its ecumenical commission . . . have been expressed by the ecumenical councils. They have especially stressed the indissoluble bond which exists between the true faith and eucharistic fellowship. The Orthodox Church accordingly has always striven to take with it the different churches and confessions in the common search for the lost unity of Christians, so that all arrive at the unity of faith.
>
> 6. However, the Orthodox Church, in truth to its ecclesiology, to the identity of its inner structure and, indeed, to the teaching of the undivided church, rejects the thought of an "equality of confessions" and is not able to understand the unity of the church as a balance/adjustment between confessions. In this sense the unity

44. In: *Episkepsis* no. 369 (December 1986). It is expressly mentioned that the decisions of this preconciliar conference still possess no canonical force, and this is true until the awaited Holy and Great Council expresses itself. Nevertheless, it is stressed that these decisions may be of "direct use."

sought . . . cannot simply be the result of theological agreement. God calls each Christian to the unity of faith, as it is lived in the mystery and tradition within the Orthodox Church.

All of this can be summarized in the following points of view:

- The unity of the church is not only obscured or hidden. *The unity of the church is "lost."* Loss of unity is more than division among the churches; it is division of the church (schism). The unity of the church must, therefore, not only be made "visible" but also be "regained."
- The reason for the loss of unity is that the churches have *not preserved "the tradition of the ancient, undivided church,"* that is, the tradition of the church of the first seven ecumenical councils. Unity will be regained by all these churches "returning" to the tradition of the ancient, undivided church and thereby "returning" to the church.
- This tradition of the ancient, undivided church includes in itself the *apostolic faith,* the *sacramental life,* especially the eucharistic life, and the *ministry,* understood as the episcopate standing in apostolic succession and the sacramental priesthood. The effort for unity and consensus must concentrate on each of these elements.
- However, these constitutive elements of the tradition of the ancient, undivided church — and with it the unity of the church — are seen as *one indivisible whole*. They are so inseparably and intimately connected that they can never be taken individually. The loss of one of these elements means ultimately the loss of all, and each of the elements is really only preserved if all elements are preserved.
- Only in the Orthodox Church is the tradition of the undivided church preserved in its wholeness and integrity. The *Orthodox Church is the preserver of this tradition,* and only in it is this tradition, and with it the church in its unity, a living, lived, and visible reality.

2.2.5. The Roman Catholic Church

In order to describe the Roman Catholic understanding of church unity with the help of ecclesiastically binding doctrinal statements, one can refer not to texts of the past but rather to those of the present. At the fifth public session of the Second Vatican Council on November 21, 1964, the "Dogmatic Constitution on the Church" *(Lumen gentium)* and the "Decree on Ecumenism" *(Unitatis redintegratio)* were promulgated. The first chapter of the latter,[45] which is entitled "Catholic Principles of Ecumenism" and constantly refers to Holy Scripture and the ecclesiastical doctrinal tradition, developed the Roman Catholic understanding of the unity of the church.

The first part of that chapter[46] is especially important. A strong emphasis on the Spirit follows a Christological substantiation of unity that is placed into a trinitarian and salvation-historical framework,[47] and a reference to the Eucharist "by which the unity of the Church is both signified and brought about." The Spirit is the "principle of the Church's unity" because the Spirit binds the faithful in Christ and thus "brings about that wonderful communion of the faithful" *(communio fidelium)*. In this the "basic ecumenical conviction" and the "ecumenical indicative" (cf. 2.1.2.) are underscored in all clarity.[48]

Only then is there a reference to the college of the twelve apostles, especially to Peter, to whom (the apostles) Christ "has entrusted the office of teaching, supervision, and sanctification." Thus, the text leads to the concise, and for our context especially important, statement about the church and its unity.

> It is through the faithful preaching of the Gospel by the Apostles and their successors — the bishops with Peter's successor as their head — through their administrating the sacraments, and through their governing in love, that Jesus Christ wishes his people to increase under the action of the holy Spirit; and he perfects its fellowship in unity: in their confession of one faith, in the common cele-

45. *UR*, 2–4.

46. *UR*, 2.

47. "In this the love of God was made manifest among us, that the Father sent his only-begotten Son into the world so that becoming human, he might by his redemption give new life and unity to the entire human race" (*UR*, 2).

48. This is also in the *Catechism of the Catholic Church*. See No. 813.

bration of divine worship, and in the fraternal harmony of the family of God.

The "Three Visible Bonds" of Ecclesiastical Unity

Three elements that are constitutive for the life and unity of the church are highlighted here in an interesting doubling that provides a particular emphasis.

1. the "faithful (*fidelis,* that is, corresponding to the one and true faith) preaching of the gospel";
2. the "administration of the sacraments," to which the predicate *"fidelis"* refers in like manner, both grammatically and materially;
3. the governance *(gubernatio)* by the bishops as the successors of the apostles with the successor of Peter as their head.

In the second part of this section this corresponds to:

1. the communion in the confession of the one faith;
2. the "common celebration of the divine liturgy," which means in particular the celebration of the Eucharist;
3. the "brotherly/sisterly harmony of God's family," which, according to Catholic understanding, always includes the office of governance, the pastoral office, whose task it is to take care of this harmony.[49]

This corresponds to the traditional Catholic view of the *"tria vincula,"*[50] the three visible bonds of fellowship[51] through which the unity of the church is preserved. Other texts of Vatican II also include this reference.[52] Indeed, this traditional view stands today in

49. In one of the preconciliar drafts instead of *"in familiae Dei fraterna concordia"* it reads *"in regiminis pastorum fraterna concordia."*

50. *Vinculum symbolicum, vinculum liturgicum, vinculum sociale vel hierarchicum.* See, e.g., Y. M. Congar in *Mysal* IV/1: 372–95; esp. 372–75.

51. *Catechism,* No. 815, and also Catholic Church. Pontificium Consilium ad Christianorum Unitatem Fovendam, *Directory for the Application of Principles and Norms on Ecumenism,* no. 12 (Washington, D.C.: U.S. Catholic Conference, 1993).

52. *Lumen gentium* (in the following cited as *LG*) 14: Decree on the Catholic Oriental Churches *(Orientalium Ecclesiarum)* 2.

the framework of a trinitarian, and especially pneumatologically intensified, understanding of the nature of the church.[53]

The first two constitutive elements of ecclesiastical unity basically coincide with what is upheld by the Reformation and Anglican churches. Unity of the church requires the agreement in the true faith, otherwise there can be fellowship neither in the preaching of the gospel nor in the administration of the sacraments. Therefore, the effort for unity includes as an essential aspect the theological effort for consensus in the understanding of the faith. This is stressed as much by the Catholic Church as it is by the Reformation churches.

The Catholic position, however — like the Anglican understanding of unity but differing from that of the Reformation — includes the explicit mention of the ecclesiastical office (ministry).

Episcopate and Papacy

Just as in the case of the Anglican understanding of unity, here it is also a question of the *office of bishop,* derived from the office of the apostles and in continuous historical succession with it. The importance of the episcopate, however, is even more decisive here. It is not merely added as yet another element of unity to the other elements of unity; it also determines them. For the bishops have the "ministry for the communion" *(communitatis ministerium),* and they exercise this ministry in a threefold respect: as "teachers of doctrine, ministers of sacred worship, and holders of office in government."[54] Therefore, each individual item of these three elements of unity — the "confession of the one faith," the "celebration of the divine liturgy," and the "harmony" — cannot be separated from the episcopate. The bishops are also the "visible source and foundation of the unity" *(visibile principium et fundamentum . . . unitatis)* for their local churches and their life in each respect.[55] Once this is seen, it becomes clear why from the Catholic side there is no discussion and seeking of the unity of the church apart from the episcopate.

53. Cf. *Catechism,* Nos. 813 and 815.

54. *LG* 20. Each individual task of the three tasks of bishops is described one after the other in chapter III of the Constitution of the Church from Vatican II. That chapter as a whole especially deals with the office of bishop (*LG* 25, 26, 27).

55. *LG* 23.

From this comprehensive unifying function of the bishops, the papal office and its importance, according to Catholic thinking, for the unity of the church must be understood. It is true that the individual bishops are the "visible principle and foundation of the unity of their particular churches" or of the local church that they oversee. But what about the unity between the local or particular churches and, therefore, the unity of the universal church? The Roman Catholic answer refers not only to the fellowship, the "college" of bishops, but also always to the primacy of the Bishop of Rome, the successor of Peter. It also refers to the special place of Peter in the college of apostles, the place which Christ has assigned to him.

> In order that the episcopate itself, however, might be one and undivided, he [Christ] put Peter at the head of the apostles, and in him he set up a lasting and visible source and foundation of the unity both of the faith and of communion.[56]

According to Roman Catholic teaching, the primacy of the Bishop of Rome is not an additional, so to say fourth, bond of unity next to the office of bishop and to the first two. Rather, the Bishop of Rome belongs to the college of bishops as its head and guarantees its indivisibility. This is one of the important ecclesiological clarifications that the Second Vatican Council has made in "continuity"[57] with previous concepts, especially those determined by Vatican I. The Constitution on the Church deals with it in its third chapter.

According to Catholic conviction, the papacy — as the continuation of the primacy of Peter — together with the office of bishop is indispensable for the unity of the church. At the same time, it can certainly be said today that this Petrine office must not everywhere and always have the same form that it has found in the Roman Catholic Church.[58]

56. *LG* 18, cf. 23.

57. *LG* 18.

58. This means, e.g., in the "Document (of the Congregation for the Doctrine of the Faith) to the Bishops of the Catholic Church Concerning Some Aspects of the Church as Communio" of May 28, 1992, that "the Petrine office irrespective of the substance, unchangeable by virtue of its divine institution, can be expressed in different ways according to its local and temporal relations . . ." (No. 18 in *OR* 22 Jahrgang, no. 25; XXIII).

The Unity of the Church Already "Existing" in the Roman Catholic Church

Because, according to the Catholic understanding of unity, all necessary "visible bonds of communion" are already fully present in the Roman Catholic Church, the Catholic understanding of unity is that, indeed, the visible unity of the church is already realized in the Roman Catholic Church. The Decree on Ecumenism declares:

> This unity, we believe, subsists *(subsistit)* in the Catholic Church as something she can never lose, and we hope that it will continue to increase until the end of time.[59]

The "Ecumenical Directory" (1993) stresses the importance of this conviction:

> Catholics hold the firm conviction that the one church of Christ subsists in the Catholic Church, "which is governed by the successor of Peter and the bishops in communion with him" (*Lumen gentium* 8)" and it adds ". . . this firm conviction and confession of faith must always be kept in mind," where Catholics strive for fellowship with other churches and speak of these churches as "churches and ecclesial communities."[60]

The observation of this Catholic conviction is in fact important in several respects:

First, it explains the Catholic reserve vis-à-vis reference to this unity as "visible unity." This is certainly not a rejection of the effort for visible unity.[61] There is, however, the concern that the understanding of this determination of the ecumenical aim could put in question the conviction that this unity already exists in the Catholic Church.

Second, this conviction implies a specific point of view about the ecumenical problem as well as a special ecumenical claim of the

59. *UR,* 4. This corresponds to the statement of the Constitution on the Church that "the one, holy, catholic, and apostolic church has *(subsistit)* its concrete form in the Catholic Church" (*LG* 8).

60. Cf. no. 17.

61. In *UR,* 1, it states regarding the ecumenical movement: "Yet almost all [churches], though in different ways, long for the one visible church of God. . . ."

Roman Catholic Church. The ecumenical problem lies in the separation "from full communion with the Catholic Church."[62] For that reason, the ecumenical aim is described consistently as "restoration of unity" *(redintegratio unitatis),* although no longer as a return to the Roman Catholic Church.[63]

Yet the conviction that the one church of Christ "'subsists' in the Catholic Church" reveals, at the same, the perspective on the ecclesial character of other churches. For the word "subsists" carries a special connotation in that Vatican II explicitly sought to say more than a mere "is." As in the Constitution on the Church, where "subsists" is first encountered and where it replaces the original "is,"[64] Vatican II wants to acknowledge that many and significant elements of the church and its unity also exist in other Christian faith-communities. In relation to the Catholic Church, one may speak accordingly of a gradient of those communities as "churches" or "ecclesial communities."

2.2.6. The Problem of "Unity and Diversity" in the Traditional Understanding of Unity

Different forms of the one Christian message and the one Christian faith arose when the original community embraced the mission to gentiles and the extension of Christianity beyond the cultural area of Jewish Palestine. From its beginnings Christianity has thus confronted the problem of "unity and diversity." The New Testament canon in its unity and variety is itself a witness to this problematic. The early Christian debate regarding these problems was of decisive importance.

The basic resolution is reflected in the account of what is commonly referred to as the "apostolic council" (Acts 15). The initial issue was — in formal terms — how to differentiate in this fundamental decision between "the essential" (cf. Acts 15:28), which, when adhered to, keeps the community of faith intact, and "the nonessential," wherein Christian freedom reigns and diversity is neither able

62. *UR,* 3.
63. *UR,* 1.
64. *LG* 8.

nor allowed to dissolve that community. If other theological considerations are left aside for the moment, this distinction provides the understanding of the church's unity as a "unity in diversity" and affirms it in principle.

How far do traditional and specifically confessional understandings of church unity take this principle into account?

The Reformation/Anglican and the Catholic Views — Difference and Commonality

The position of the Reformation churches and the Anglican Church is fundamentally clear. Their understanding of the unity of the church includes the rejection of the demand for strong uniformity and hence the affirmation of possible diversity. This is even more true for the free churches. The statement of Article 7 of the Augsburg Confession expresses this in a brief form and can represent all these churches:[65] "it is not necessary for the true unity of the church that ceremonies instituted by human beings (Latin: *traditiones humanae seu ritus ab hominibus instituti*) should be observed uniformly in all places." This is preceded by the assertion about what is necessary for the true unity of the church and what is sufficient: "For it is sufficient *(satis est)* for the true unity of the Christian church that the gospel be preached with pure understanding of it and the sacraments be administered in accordance with the divine Word."

The distinction between what is essential and what is nonessential for unity is thus safeguarded with great emphasis. It follows in principle the criterion whether something is "transmitted by the Lord in Scripture," "the divine Word," or "according to Christ's ordinance," or whether it is only "instituted by human beings," "transmitted by human laws," or based on the peculiarity of the "countries, times, and human customs."[66] This distinction between essential and nonessential is a distinguishing mark of the Reforma-

65. Cf. the Second Helvetic Confession, 17, and Article 34 of the Anglican "Thirty-nine Articles" (see 2.2.1. and 2.2.2.).

66. The citations refer to the statements of the Augsburg Confession, the Second Helvetic Confession, and the "Thirty-nine Articles" cited above (2.2.1. and 2.2.2.).

tion and the Anglican understanding of the church and its unity. Behind this distinction stands the fundamental concern of the sixteenth-century Reformation (cf. 2.2.1.).

The emphatic nature with which the churches of the Reformation represented this distinction over against the Roman Catholic Church of their time cannot conceal the fact that the differentiation between essential and nonessential was also maintained in principle by Catholicism in spite of ever-present countertendencies.[67] The response of the "Confutatio" to the statement of the Augsburg Confession (Article 7) may be taken in this context as a relevant example. It expressly acknowledges that "the difference of rites *(rituum varietas)* does not divide the unity of the faith."[68]

This Catholic response, however, also clearly shows the difference from the view of the Reformation. The criterion of apostolicity — and with it the criterion of whether something is "from the Lord" and thus necessary — is defined differently than by the Reformation. Not only is reference made to Holy Scripture or to the Word of God, but a demonstration is also provided with regard to universal validity in the church.[69]

This difference between the Reformation and the Catholic understanding is doubtless of considerable consequence as soon as one must demonstrate in detail what is essential and what is nonessential for the unity of the church. It does not abrogate the fact, how-

67. Cf. Y. Congar, *Diversités et communion. Dossier historique et conclusion théologique* (Paris: 1982), esp. the chapter entitled *"Des diversités ont toujours été admises dans l'unité de la foi"*, 37-54. The Reformers also were conscious that they stood with their distinction completely in the tradition of the church. The reference of the Second Helvetic Confession, "that in the ancient writers there was a manifold diversity of rites *(ritus),* but that they were free, and no one ever thought that the unity of the church was thereby dissolved," is found in similar form also in the Lutheran Confessions (*CA,* 26; *BSLK,* 106f.; *Formula of Concord, Solid Declaration,* 10; esp. *BSLK,* 1063; cf. Apology 7, *BSLK,* 241–46).

68. Herbert Immenkötter, ed., *Die Confutatio der Confessio Augustana vom 3. August 1530,* Corpus Catholicorum, vols. 33, 96, and 97 (Münster, Westfalen: Aschendorf, 1979).

69. In this sense, the Confutation concedes only the diversity of particular church rites; but it demands agreement in universal church rites and ceremonies *(universales ecclesiae ritus)* with the reasoning that "it is to be assumed that they come from the apostles." Exactly this argumentation of the Confutation, which is completely in the sense of the canon of Vincent of Lerins, is disputed by the Apology of the Augsburg Confession (Apology 7, 38ff., *BSLK,* 244f.).

ever, that this distinction between essential and nonessential is found in principle on both sides. The Decree on Ecumenism confirms this and states:

> While preserving unity in essentials, let everyone in the Church, according to the office entrusted to him, preserve a proper freedom in the various forms of spiritual life and discipline, in the variety of liturgical rites, and even in the theological elaborations of revealed truth. In all things let charity prevail.[70]

Legitimate Diversity Also in Doctrinal Teaching

It is characteristic of both the traditional Reformation and the Catholic understanding that permissible diversity is accepted primarily in the area of ecclesiastical usages, practices, ceremonies, rites, and rules. On the other hand, doctrinal teaching is excluded as an area of permissible diversity. Here the need for agreement is constantly stressed.[71]

Nevertheless, one continually encounters the awareness that the distinction between essential and nonessential can and must be applied also to the area of doctrinal teaching. This can occur in two ways: first, as the distinction between *"verba"* and *"res,"* that is, between the linguistic form of the doctrine, which can be varied, and the actual content of the doctrine, in which there is need of agree-

70. *UR,* 4. In paraphrased form, the dictum is accepted here: *"In necessariis unitas, in non necessariis libertas, in omnibus caritas,"* which clearly has its roots in Augustine and the church fathers, but which in this form appears to be of Lutheran origin (Rupertus Meldenius [1626] *"Si nos servaremus in necessariis unitatem, in non necessariis libertatem, in utrisque charitatem, opitimo certe loco essent res nostrae."* Cf. Y. Congar [footnote 67 above], 156f.). The use of this dictum on both the Catholic and Reformation side reveals once more the commonality of the fundamental distinction between essential and nonessential.

71. This is shown already in Article 7 of the Augsburg Confession and in its Reformed and Anglican equivalents. This also corresponds to Catholic thought. For example, Luther repeatedly emphasizes and comments regarding the Confession of the Czech Brethren that even though uniformity and unanimity are not needed in the area of the church's customs and rites, they are necessary in the area of doctrine and morals (*WA* 50, 380). The *"doctrina fidei et morum"* permits no diversity. *"Haec enim debet esse eadem"* (cf. *WA.B* 7, 176, and 177). This view is fully shared by Catholics and Orthodox.

ment; second, as the distinction between "fundamental" and "nonfundamental" articles of faith or doctrinal teaching.

One could say that on the whole the Reformation churches have been more open to this distinction than the Catholic Church. The distinction between the linguistic form *("verba")* and the actual content *("res")* of doctrinal teaching is found in all its clearness in Luther.[72] He and the Reformers also distinguish between articles of faith that are fundamental, less fundamental, or not fundamental at all.[73] This form of making distinctions is developed further soon after the Reformation into a regular teaching on "fundamental articles" — partly in line with the thinking of Erasmus of Rotterdam — by Lutheran, Reformed, and eventually also Anglican theologians.[74] This doctrine became of secondary importance in Lutheran and Reformed circles after the seventeenth century, but it remains in many respects determinative in Anglicanism.[75]

72. Again reference can be made here to Luther's comments on the confession of the Czech Brethren. There he always distinguishes between the "language" and the "object" or between "word and expression" and "meaning and thought" (*WA,* 38, 78f.; *WA.B,* 7, 176, and 177). Agreement in the "object" *(res ipsa)* or in "meaning and thought" *(sensus et sententia)* is what is decisive and necessary. It alone is ultimately that which preserves the necessary unity of faith. *"Verum . . . frustra de verbis disceptatur, ubi res ipsae conveniunt"* (*WA.B,* 7, 176).

73. It appears in the structure and construction of the individual confessional writings, e.g., the Augsburg Confession with its twofold division into "the chief articles of faith" and "the abuses" that need to be abolished, or in Luther's Smalcald Articles, which work with three categories of doctrinal articles: the noncontroversial trinitarian and Christological articles, controversial articles absolutely requiring clarification, and finally such articles about which there can be an academic discussion. With Calvin, the matter is even clearer: He distinguishes between "essential" and "properly doctrinal matters" and "other doctrinal matters, concerning which diversities of thought prevail among the churches, but which do not break the unity of the church" (*Institutio* IV, 1, 12; cf. 2, 1).

74. On the doctrine of fundamental articles, cf., e.g., the article by W. Joest "Fundamentalartikel" in *TRE* vol. 11, 727–32 (Lit.).

75. On the doctrine of fundamental articles in Anglicanism, cf. S. W. Sykes, *"Die Fundamentalien des Christentums,"* in *Grundkonsens — Grunddifferenz,* ed. A. Birmele and H. Meyer (Frankfurt: O. Lembeck, 1992), 132–44. The concept of "comprehensiveness," deriving from Anglican apologetics, must be mentioned here. Originally it referred to the connection, characteristic of the Anglican tradition, of Protestant and Catholic elements. As the Lambeth Conference of 1968 stated, it further designated an Anglican "attitude of mind," arising from "the controversies of its history." "Comprehensiveness demands agreement on the funda-

The Catholic Church and the Orthodox churches have rejected the thought that in the area of ecclesiastical doctrinal teachings there are doctrines which are less binding and not essential for the unity of the faith.[76] They are, however, familiar with and are able to apply ecumenically the distinction between variable linguistic-conceptual form and enduring binding content of doctrinal teaching.[77]

2.3. Ecumenical Processes

Ecumenical Declarations About the Unity of the Church

The ecumenical movement could not rest content with diverse understandings of unity merely existing side by side. As a goal-oriented movement and for the sake of its inner cohesion and its orientation, it needed an understanding of its aim — the visible unity of the

mentals, while tolerating disagreement on matters in which Christians may differ without feeling the necessity of breaking communion" (The Lambeth Conference 1968, *Resolutions and Reports* [London: S.P.C.K., 1968], 140).

76. In the encyclical *Mortalium animos* of 1928 the distinction *"inter capita fidei fundamentalia et non fundamentalia,"* a distinction in which the first category is binding on all, and the second where free decision is left to the believers, is expressly rejected (*AAS* 20 [1928], 13f.). This still holds today, and the language of "hierarchies of truths" of the Decree on Ecumenism (*UR,* 11) certainly does not want to introduce this distinction (cf. the Declaration of the Congregation for the Doctrine of the Faith, "On the Catholic Teaching of the Church which is to provide a defence against some present errors" [*Mysterium ecclesiae*], 1973, No. 4). The Orthodox rejection of such a distinction is stated, e.g., in the declaration of the Orthodox delegates to the Assembly of the World Council of Churches in Evanston (1954): "The whole of the Christian faith should be regarded as one indivisible unity. It is not enough to accept just certain particular doctrines, basic as they may be in themselves. . . . We cannot accept a rigid distinction between essential and non-essential doctrines. . . ." See G. Patelos, ed., *The Orthodox Church,* 94.

77. When the Decree on Ecumenism says "maintain a proper freedom . . . even in their theological elaborations of revealed truth," this is nothing new but rather a statement deeply anchored in the Catholic tradition (*UR,* 4). It was precisely the popes of the last two decades — Paul VI and John Paul II — who in several common declarations together with patriarchs of Eastern Orthodox churches have repeatedly used this distinction between "faith" and "theological means of expression" or between "identity" or "substance of faith" and "difference in terminology." They have thus shown that both traditions, the Roman Catholic and the Orthodox, are familiar with this distinction.

church — that was as clear as possible and enjoyed consensus in relation to its basic tenets.

The way to such a common understanding of unity, however, appeared to be made more difficult for the World Council of Churches by the "Toronto Declaration" of 1950, which, among other things, addressed the matter of the "ecclesiological neutrality" of the WCC. It stated that "Membership in the World Council does not imply the acceptance of a specific doctrine concerning the nature of church unity."[78]

2.3.1. The Declaration of Unity of New Delhi and Its Significance

Without violating the ecclesiological neutrality of the World Council of Churches and in "continuity" with the Toronto Declaration, the Faith and Order Commission succeeded in developing a "formula of unity," which describes the characteristics and, at the same time, the requirements for the visible unity of the church being sought. It was accepted by the World Council Assembly in New Delhi (1961) and explained in a commentary. It reads:

> We believe that the unity which is both God's will and his gift to his Church is being made visible as all in each place who are baptized into Jesus Christ and confess him as Lord and Saviour are brought by the Holy Spirit into one fully committed fellowship, holding the one apostolic faith, preaching the one Gospel, breaking the one bread, joining in common prayer, and having a corporate life reaching out in witness and service to all and who at the same time are united with the whole Christian fellowship in all places and ages in such wise that ministry and members are accepted by all, and that all can act and speak together as occasion requires for the tasks to which God calls his people. It is for such a unity that we believe we must pray and work.[79]

78. Toronto Declaration. See Kinnamon and Cope, eds., *The Ecumenical Movement,* 465.

79. As stated in the Report of Section II of the World Council Assembly in New Delhi, 117–18.

The New Delhi declaration of unity was a decisive step, which cannot be estimated highly enough for the development of the ecumenical movement. For the first time the various ecumenical intentions and particular concerns were compressed into a common, almost confessional statement that described the unity sought (a) in its nature and (b) in its different constitutive elements and thereby in its multidimensionality.

Attention to this *multidimensionality of the unity sought* is of the greatest importance for the ecumenical effort, and the enduring contribution of the Assembly at New Delhi is that its declaration of unity and its accompanying commentary articulated this, even if subsequent development of the understanding of unity developed more clearly several of these points.[80] The following appertain to unity of the church being sought:

- Agreement in the confession of the faith and mutuality in the sacraments and in the ecclesiastical office (ministry),
- Common worship life and prayer,
- Common witness and common service to all human beings,
- The ability to act and speak together in view of concrete tasks and challenges,
- The local as well as the universal dimension of ecclesiastical unity,
- Unity as well as diversity.

All these belong together, and together they comprise the visible unity of the church. None is allowed to be lacking or to regard itself as absolute. None is allowed to stifle the other or to become stunted in its shadow.

All later declarations of unity, both within and outside the World Council, stand, so to speak, on the shoulders of this first declaration of unity. As has often been said and as will be shown below, these subsequent declarations constitute important explications or expansions of specific aspects of the New Delhi declaration. They do not simply abandon New Delhi, however, but rather remain fundamentally committed to it.

80. New Delhi, 116–17.

a. Unity of the Church as "Fully Committed Fellowship"

The declaration begins with statements about the nature of ecclesiastical unity, and the commentary develops these statements.[81] It is basically the recapitulation of those three fundamental and common convictions (see 2.1.), which bind together the traditional understandings of the unity of the church despite their diversities:

- The unity of the church is "God's will" — this is the "basic ecumenical conviction" from which the ecumenical movement arises (see 2.1.1.).
- The unity of the church is "God's gift" — this is the "ecumenical indicative" from which all ecumenical endeavor arises and which makes it possible and sustains it (see 2.1.2.).
- The unity of the church must become "visible" — this is the "ecumenical imperative," which sets the aim of the ecumenical effort (see 2.1.3.).

These three statements now lead to that concept, which, as no other, describes the sought after visible unity of the church in its quality: the concept of *"fellowship"* specified by the predicate *"fully committed."* The commentary indicates that it is not dealing here with a general sociological concept. At issue is quite specifically the use and adoption of the biblical and early church concept of *"koinonia/communio"* in its specific ecclesiological meaning.[82]

This concept "fellowship" appears from now on in all important declarations of unity. In the last few years, the concept of *koinonia* has largely replaced the concept of "fellowship" and has become a dominant and continually developing ecumenical leitmotif. This must, however, not obscure the fact that it has long been significant in the ecumenical movement and its understanding of the church's unity and that its essential aspects at least have been clearly outlined since New Delhi.[83] The commentary on the concept of "fully com-

81. New Delhi, 118.

82. The usual English concept of "fellowship" threatens to conceal this. Therefore, in recent times it is more often replaced by "communio" (communion) or "koinonia."

83. For further information see the following section 2.3.2.4.

mitted fellowship" stresses above all three aspects that are indicated in the following excerpt by italics.

> The word "fellowship" (koinonia) has been chosen because it describes what the Church truly is. *"Fellowship"* clearly implies that the Church is not merely an institution or organization. It is a fellowship of those who are called together by the Holy Spirit and in baptism confess Christ as Lord and Saviour. They are thus *"fully committed"* to him and to one another. Such a fellowship means for those who participate in it nothing less than a renewed mind and spirit, a full participation in common praise and prayer, the shared realities of penitence and forgiveness, mutuality in suffering and joy, listening together to the same Gospel, responding in faith, obedience and service, joining in the one mission of Christ in the world, a self-forgetting love for all for whom Christ died, and the reconciling grace which breaks down every wall of race, colour, caste, tribe, sex, class, and nation. Neither does this *"fellowship"* imply a rigid uniformity of structure, organization, or government. A lively variety marks corporate life in the one Body of one Spirit.[84]

Each of these three aspects was developed even more clearly after New Delhi. Their basic lines, however, were already clearly discernible.

Understanding the unity of the church as "fellowship/koinonia" means:

First, it is a reflection of the fellowship with Christ, that is, it consists not simply in that Christians come together to form a communion. Rather, it consists fundamentally in that they have communion with Christ in faith, and from this — on the basis of their communion with Christ — they also have communion with one another.[85]

84. New Delhi, 119.

85. As early as the World Council Assembly in Evanston (1954), the koinonia concept was used in this sense. "Thus the communion *(koinonia)* that the members of the Church have is not simply human fellowship; it is communion with the Father and with His Son Jesus Christ through the Holy Spirit and communion with the saints in the Church triumphant" (85). Moreover, we see here what applies to New Delhi (119) and particularly for the present understanding of koinonia, namely that the Christological grounding of koinonia, when it is correctly understood, is always embedded in the Trinity.

Second, like their communion with Christ, the communion of Christians with one another is a "fully committed fellowship," not a mere aggregation but a mutual dedication and participation without reservation and boundaries.

Finally, this fully committed fellowship, nevertheless, does not mean standardization, but rather is characterized by diversity.

b. The Constitutive Elements of Ecclesiastical Unity

The New Delhi declaration was, and remained, a signpost also in that it named, and in its commentary explained in more detail, those elements that belong constitutively to the visible unity of the church in the sense of a "fully committed fellowship" and on which, therefore, ecumenical effort must be concentrated:

- mutual recognition of baptism,[86]
- common confession of the apostolic faith and common proclamation of the gospel,
- common celebration of the Lord's Supper,
- common devotional worship, petition, intercession, and thanksgiving,[87]
- common life in witness (mission) and service in the world,[88]
- mutual recognition of ministries and members,
- ability to act and speak together in view of concrete tasks and challenges.[89]

The naming of these "constitutive elements" of the visible unity of the church forms a framework that in principle includes what the traditional understandings of unity require as necessary for unity. At the same time, room remains to represent and to give accent to specifically confessional concerns.

In later declarations of unity or in similar ecumenical statements, the elements named in New Delhi return constantly. This

86. Cf. Commentary, New Delhi, 118–19.
87. Cf. Commentary, New Delhi, 120–21.
88. Cf. Commentary, New Delhi, 121.
89. Cf. Commentary, New Delhi, 128–129.

may occur with or without explicit reference to the New Delhi declaration and occasionally in another sequence or in a more condensed form.[90]

This is true also for the very concise list of the "four basic requirements" for the unity of the church as they have often appeared since the Assembly of the World Council in Nairobi (1975) (see 2.3.2.): (1) The ending of prejudices and hatreds and the lifting of condemnations; (2) communion in the one faith; (3) mutual recognition of baptism, Eucharist, and ministry; (4) agreement in how to reach decisions and compromises together.[91] The ecumenical experiences and developments reflected here — without diminishing the enduring importance of the New Delhi declaration — have led to something akin to its further extension.

2.3.2. Developments in the Understanding of Unity

The striving for a correct determination of the aim of the ecumenical movement has not ceased since New Delhi. It has continued against the background of new ecumenical developments and experiences, both within and outside the World Council of Churches: in the framework of the Commission on Faith and Order, at assemblies of the World Council of Churches, and in the Christian world communions.[92]

In the course of such developments, declarations of unity have emerged that are comparable formally to the New Delhi statement, for example, the declaration of the Commission on Faith and Order in Salamanca (1973) on the unity of the church as "conciliar

90. Cf. the World Council Assemblies in Nairobi (1975), Vancouver (1983), and Canberra (1991); see the reports of these assemblies. It is true as well for the declaration of the Lutheran World Federation "The Unity We Seek," in *Report of the Seventh Assembly of the Lutheran World Federation* (Budapest: 1984). See *LWF Report* no. 19/20 (1985), 175-76.

91. Cf., e.g., the first forum on Bilaterals (1978) in Forum on Bilateral Conversations, *The Three Reports of the Forum on Bilateral Conversations,* Faith and Order Paper no. 107 (Geneva: World Council of Churches, 1981), 8f.

92. "Christian world communions" has been the designation employed since 1980 for worldwide churches and confessional church communions, which previously were designated "confessional families" or "confessional world federations."

fellowship,"[93] which was received by the next assembly in Nairobi (1974),[94] the declaration of the Lutheran World Federation (cf. 2.3.1. and footnote 90), or the declaration of the Assembly in Canberra (1991) about "The Unity of the Church as Koinonia: Gift and Calling."[95]

The basic continuity in terms of substance, however, is always with the New Delhi declaration, which remains — expressly or implicitly — the departure and reference point. The issue is not to define the ecumenical aim anew, but to "determine in greater detail," to "describe more completely,"[96] and to "develop further"[97] the aim as it is outlined in the New Delhi declaration.

What is the content of these newer determinations or further developments of the ecumenical aim of the church's visible unity?

They can be described in terms of four approaches, the sequence of which also reflects the chronological process: (1) stress on the universal dimension of ecclesiastical unity and on the diversity inherent in unity; (2) greater attention to the structures required for unity; (3) emphasis on the mission of the church; (4) stress on the idea of koinonia.

93. World Council of Churches. Commission on Faith and Order, *What Kind of Unity?,* Faith and Order Paper no. 69 (Geneva: World Council of Churches, 1974), 121.

94. In the report from Nairobi (1975). World Council of Churches. Assembly (5th: 1975: Nairobi, Kenya), *Breaking Barriers, Nairobi 1975: The Official Report of the Fifth Assembly of the World Council of Churches, Nairobi, 23 November–10 December, 1975* (London: Published in collaboration with the World Council of Churches by SPCK; Grand Rapids: Eerdmans, 1976), 59–66 (in the following cited as Nairobi).

95. In the report from Canberra. *Official Report of the Seventh Assembly of the World Council of Churches* (Geneva: 1991), 172–74 (in the following cited as Canberra).

96. E.g., in the Assembly of the World Council of Churches in Nairobi. See Nairobi, 59–60.

97. In referring back to the preceding declarations as those of New Delhi and Nairobi, the Assembly of Vancouver stated: "This view of the aim clearly will and should be further developed." Report from Vancouver (1983). *Official Report of the Sixth Assembly of the World Council of Churches* (Geneva: World Council of Churches, 1983), 44 (in the following cited as Vancouver).

2.3.2.1. The Universal Dimension of Unity and the Value of Diversity

"All in each place" — with this formula the New Delhi declaration expressly stressed the local dimension, the "here and now" of ecclesiastical unity and of the ecumenical effort. If the unity of the church is to become visible and capable of being experienced, then this must happen especially where Christians meet and live together in concrete vocational, social, and national relations. The commentary states: "in each school," "in each factory or office," "in each congregation," but then also between the congregations and in the respective states and nations, in which Christians live together.[98]

This certainly does not overlook, however, the local and time-transcending dimension of ecclesiastical unity, that is, the unity "of the whole Christian communion in all places and all ages," as the last part of the New Delhi declaration states. Nevertheless, it appeared necessary to pay even greater attention to this universal dimension of ecclesiastical unity and to stress that the unity of the church exceeds and encompasses individual and varying "places," countries, and national or cultural areas. Impulses for this resulted from menacing global-social as well as economic developments, but also from the ecumenical movement itself, especially from the new and intensified ecumenical engagement of the churches of the Third World and the Christian world communions and, not least, the Roman Catholic Church.

The "Catholicity" of the Church and of Its Unity

The emphasis on this universal dimension of the church and its unity characterized the Assembly of the World Council of Churches in Uppsala (1968) and what it said about the ecumenical aim.[99]

The leitmotif was "catholicity." It was to refer to a "deeper, inter-

98. New Delhi, 118.

99. Especially in the report of section I, "The Holy Spirit and the Catholicity of the Church," in World Council of Churches. Assembly (4th: 1968: Uppsala, Sweden), *The Uppsala Report 1968: Official Report of the Fourth Assembly of the World Council of Churches* (Geneva: World Council of Churches, 1968), 11–19 (in the following cited as Uppsala).

nal dimension" of unity.[100] Unity of the church means certainly a denial of that which separates. In its inner core, however, it means affirmation: affirmation of the "fullness, the integrity, and the totality of life in Christ" made real by the Spirit.[101] Divisions are, therefore, ultimately "denials" of this catholicity;[102] they are forms of "egoism and particularism." And the effort for the visible unity of the church is the struggle to give expression to the catholicity of the church, that is, its "integrity and totality."[103]

This is developed in four respects: as "the quest for diversity," "the quest for continuity," "the quest for the unity of the whole church," and "the quest for the unity of humankind." Here the first three parts — in reverse order — are of utmost importance. All are connected to what was already mentioned in the New Delhi declaration, where it was of secondary importance but is now emphasized more strongly.

- The local dimension of unity that was stressed in New Delhi must — as it is stated in Uppsala — be supplemented by "a fresh understanding of the unity of all Christians in all places."[104] Locally oriented ecumenism, that is, one focused on the unity "in each place," is not allowed to be sufficient in itself. An effort for unity that is limited to its own narrow national and cultural "place" or context can lead to the stabilization of national and cultural boundaries that endanger the unity of the church. Therefore, both *local and universal endeavors for unity,* relating to the locality and transcending it, must go hand in hand.[105]
- The unity of the church is to be endangered just as little by temporal limitations. This unity is not bound to the present but rather is also a *unity in time.* For the church is "the one people of God in every age."[106] It is "the pilgrim people of God" wandering through history that derives "from Christ through the apostles" and "remains true to the faith and mission of the apostles"

100. Uppsala, 13.
101. Uppsala, 13.
102. Uppsala, 15.
103. Uppsala, 13.
104. Uppsala, 17.
105. Uppsala, 15.
106. Uppsala, 16.

in the change of generations and epochs. Certainly, the church is in constant need of renewal, but it stands, at the same time, under the demand for "continuity."[107] Because the unity of the church possesses this dimension of temporal universality, "the quest for continuity" belongs to the quest for unity.

"The Quest for Diversity"

Where the understanding of the unity of the church includes this dimension of "catholicity," of the universal totality, fullness, and integrity of the church, diversity and difference in the life of the church are cast in a new light. In the first instance, they no longer appear as a threat to unity. Rather they can be conceived as essential marks of unity. They can be a manifestation of "dynamic catholicity," that is, "the expression of the apostolic calling of the church" and thus testify to the one apostolic faith, so that this witness extends to all the world in its many diverse forms.[108] In this light, diversity is no longer treated immediately with an ecumenical reservation but becomes an ecumenical imperative. The quest for unity is "the quest for diversity." As a result, the old and constantly recurring ecumenical maxim that "unity does not mean uniformity"[109] is turned into something positive. And the statement of New Delhi, that a "lively variety" is a characteristic of Christian fellowship or koinonia, is also further developed.

These new accentuations that became incorporated into the understanding of unity particularly at Uppsala are not going to disappear again. They have held their own since then and have in fact become more pronounced, both in relation to the universal dimension of unity and even more so in relation to a new assessment of diversity.

- In view of the *universal dimension of unity that transcends the local,* one must pose the question, How can this "unity of all Chris-

107. Uppsala, 16.

108. Uppsala, 15.

109. This was already the case at the first World Conference on Faith and Order in Lausanne (1927). See H. N. Bate, ed., *The World Conference on Faith and Order* (London: 1927), e.g., 466.

tians in all places" that was stressed at Uppsala take on form and be portrayed? Is mere aggregation and togetherness of local congregations and of regional and national churches that mutually recognize one another sufficient? Or does not this universal unity of the churches need a structured form that corresponds to it, so that unity can become visible and a common speech and action of all churches become possible?

The answer, which was already apparent in Uppsala,[110] is clearly given at the next Assembly of the World Council at Nairobi (1975): "The one Church is to be envisioned as *a conciliar fellowship of local churches*. . . ."[111] The one, universal church thus should portray itself as "conciliar," that is, in conciliar gatherings and assemblies of representatives of the individual churches. This is its public, structural form. This will be discussed in more detail later (see 3.3.1.4.). Here it is sufficient to note how attention to the universal dimension of ecclesiastical unity has been maintained after Uppsala and even strengthened.

- This is even more the case in relation to the *renewed assessment of diversity*. What had been stated in Uppsala on this subject was fully received at Nairobi (1975). Statements are made about a "unity which does not impose uniformity upon desirable diversity,"[112] and there were comments about the idea of "conciliar fellowship": "It underlines the fact that true unity is not monolithic, does not override the special gifts given to each member and to each local church, but rather cherishes and protects them."[113] The trinitarian perspective, in which the unity of the church has been seen especially since New Delhi,[114] is defined in this sense: "It is because the unity of the church is grounded in the divine trinity that we can speak of diversity in the Church as something to be not only admitted but actively desired."[115]

110. Uppsala, 17.
111. Nairobi, 60.
112. Nairobi, 59.
113. Nairobi, 60.
114. New Delhi, 7.
115. Nairobi, 61.

The positive assessment of diversity resurfaces again at the Assembly of the World Council of Churches in Vancouver (1983)[116] and appears with special clarity at the Assembly of the World Council of Churches in Canberra (1991), where the unity of the church is spoken of as "koinonia":

> Diversities which are rooted in theological traditions, various cultural, ethnic, or historical contacts are integral to the nature of communion. . . . In communion diversities are brought together in harmony as gifts of the Holy Spirit, contributing to the richness and fullness of the church of God.[117]

Two Kinds of Legitimate Diversity

Two kinds of diversities belong to the nature of unity as koinonia: those that are "theologically" grounded and those that are "contextually" grounded. Referring to these diversities, the Assembly of Canberra received the fruit of an important and protracted process that had characterized the seventies in particular. At issue was the question that had presented itself right at the beginning of the ecumenical movement: Are not only cultural, ethnic, and other "contextual" diversities but also "confessional-ecclesiastical" diversities part of the sought after unity, or do they have to be given up for the sake of unity? Attention will be given later to the intense debate in which the Christian world communions were engaged (see below 3.3.1. and 3.3.1.4.). Here it is important to note that already at the end of the 1970s an ecumenical consensus emerged that confessional-ecclesiastical diversities are reconcilable and could have their place as "reconciled diversities" in the unity of the church being sought. The long period that was governed by the view, championed in particular by the WCC, that the church's unity had basically to be "transconfessional" and the inherited diversity of ecclesiastical-confessional traditions be therefore left behind came to an end (3.1.2. and 3.1.3.). Already in 1984 the Lu-

116. Vancouver, 44-45. Regarding the total view of the eucharistic vision of unity developed there, it states: "Our eucharistic vision . . . tends . . . to shed new light on Christian unity in its full richness of diversity."

117. Canberra, 173.

theran World Federation had said in its declaration about unity, "The Unity We Seek":

> The diversity present in this communion rises out of the differing cultural and ethnic contexts in which the one church of Christ lives out its mission and out of the number of church traditions in which the apostolic faith has been maintained, transmitted, and lived throughout the centuries. In recognizing these diversities as expressions of the one apostolic faith and the one catholic church, traditions are changed, antagonisms overcome, and mutual condemnations lifted. The diversities are reconciled and transformed into a legitimate and indispensable multiformity within the one body of Christ.[118]

Seven years later the Assembly of the World Council of Churches in Canberra accepted this in its own way.

The ecumenical reassessment of diversity as it was employed at Uppsala has so changed the understanding of unity that today one can no longer discuss the unity of the church without considering these diversities which belong to unity and must find their place in it.[119]

2.3.2.2. Greater Attention to the Structures Required for the Unity of the Church

From its beginnings, the ecumenical movement had to deal with the question whether and how far the sought-after unity of the church must also find structural-organizational expression. For the sake of the "visibility" of unity, some emphatically represented the necessity of structures of unity. Others opposed this view and gave the necessity of structures a lower classification or even denied it.

118. See above footnote 90. At the Assembly of the Lutheran World Federation in Dar es Salaam, 1977, a declaration was provided about "models of unity" which made the case for a "unity in reconciled diversity" (in Lutheran World Federation. Assembly [6th: 1977: Dar es Salaam, Tanzania], *In Christ, A New Community: The Proceedings of the Sixth Assembly of the Lutheran World Federation, Dar-es-Salaam, Tanzania, June 13–25, 1977* [Geneva: The Federation, 1977], 173–75 and 200).

119. The theme "unity and diversity" stands thus at the center of the wider theological discussions of the 1980s about models of unity (see 3.3.3.).

This question is closely connected with the more comprehensive question of the "models of unity" to be discussed later, but it already touches the fundamental understanding of unity and even the understanding of the church as such. There were those who, looking to the concrete form of the church's unity, advocated the model of "(organic) union"; they did so because their understanding of church and church unity already included the structural element. Others whose understanding of the church and church unity excluded the structural element or gave it low priority championed the model of mutual recognition of churches, of mere pulpit and eucharistic communion, or — in the interest of cooperation among churches — the structurally "light" form of church federations or alliances.

It is hardly possible to connect these two concepts precisely with individual ecclesiastical-confessional traditions. They cross over their boundaries constantly. In view of the early ecumenical movement, however, one can still legitimately say that the churches of episcopal form stressed the structural element, while the Lutherans and certainly the free churches confronted structural shaping of ecclesiastical unity with considerable reservation, indeed, with disapproval.

Here, too, the ecumenical development of recent decades has clearly continued.

The declaration of unity of New Delhi and its commentary were still quite reserved on this point. They only say (see 2.3.1.) that it belongs to the sought-after unity "that all can act and speak together as occasion requires for the tasks to which God calls his people."

Nevertheless, the reflection on the structures required for unity sets out again and again from this point, that is, from the question of the *capacity for common action and speaking* in the face of concrete challenges. And this reflection was and is motivated by the conviction that the aim of the ecumenical movement, according to New Delhi, is a "fully committed fellowship" in faith, life, and action, and not just a mutually respected and recognized coexistence of churches. However, if this communion of churches wants to be "fully committed" in faith, life, and action, and not just on an optional and occasional basis, then it needs structural means and possibilities. Inherent in the notion of "committed fellowship" itself is the postulate that there must be structures of communion that facilitate common decision-making, acting, and speaking when and wherever such is called for.

Therefore, by declaring "that all act and speak in togetherness" to be one of the constitutive elements of "committed fellowship," the New Delhi declaration on unity has provided the point of departure for inquiry about the structures requisite for unity.

The Uppsala Assembly carried this process forward and concretized it in that from now on the *thought of conciliarity* determines more exactly the nature of the structures required for communion. The "common life" in the one church should have a "conciliar form."[120] This also holds for the Assembly in Nairobi and its description of the unity of the church as a "*conciliar fellowship* (of local churches)," a concept that as such includes the structural aspect of communion.

> They (the different local churches) are one in their common commitment to confess the gospel of Christ by proclamation and service to the world. To this end, each church aims at maintaining sustained and sustaining relationships with her sister churches, expressed in conciliar gatherings whenever required for the fulfillment of their common calling.[121]

The Assembly of Canberra (1991) in its declaration about the unity of the church as koinonia expresses it still more concisely:

> This full communion will be expressed on the local and universal levels through conciliar forms of life and action.[122]

One sees how this ecumenical process, which led to a greater attention to the structures required for unity, includes those churches that for a long time met a structured form of ecclesiastical unity with a critical reservation. This would at least be true for the Lutheran churches. In its declaration "The Unity We Seek," the Lutheran World Federation stated: The unity that is to be understood as "communion" "is ordered in all its components in conciliar structures and actions."[123]

120. Uppsala, 17.
121. Nairobi, 60.
122. Canberra, 173.
123. See above footnote 90.

Once again we emphasize that in the end it was the concept of "fully commited fellowship" or communion that, since New Delhi, has heightened attention to common structures required for unity and made for greater acceptance of this conviction than ever before. It is not a concern with structures that primarily serve an external, organizational unity of the church. Rather, it is the communion, lived in common faith, witness, and action, that calls for common structural forms in faith, life, and action, in other words, from within itself, so that this togetherness in faith may come about and be maintained. That these structures are in principle to be "conciliar" in kind similarly corresponds to the concept of fellowship or communion.

2.3.2.3. Emphasis on the Mission of the Church

As we have seen, the enduring contribution of the New Delhi declaration of unity was to articulate a multidimensional understanding of the unity of the church. Communion in the understanding of faith, in the sacraments, and in the ecclesiastical office (ministry) belongs as much to the sought-after unity as communion in mission, that is, in the missionary witness of the faith and the diaconal and social service in the world.

While the declaration of New Delhi integrates and firmly interconnects these aspects and dimensions of ecclesiastical unity — one could say the unity *"ad intra"* and the unity *"ad extra"* — it reflects what also had taken place in the ecumenical movement in terms of structure: the integration of the three historical mainstreams of the ecumenical movement, the movement of Faith and Order, the movement for practical Christianity (Life and Work), and finally also the missionary movement in the World Council of Churches.

"Church for Others" — "Unity of Humankind"

In the time after New Delhi, there was great emphasis on the "mission" of the church, that is, on its "missionary" dimension understood in a wider sense.

There was a desire to view the church in all of its being and action under the aspect of the *task that directs the church to the world.*

The church is "church for others." Here is, as it were, the criterion for the church's genuineness and the principle of its required renewal. At the same time, a changed understanding of mission — mission as participation of the church in the mission of God *(missio Dei)* aiming at the renewal of creation — allows the "missionary" commission of the church in its classical sense to move in a very close connection with its diaconal and social task. The traditional distinction between mission and diaconia, between evangelizing witness and social service, gives way to a fundamental comprehension in which, it is true, the dominant commitment is to human beings, suffering under various forms of poverty and social injustice, and for freedom, dignity, and integrity of humanity.

At the Assembly in Uppsala (1968) there was a clear expression of this understanding of church and mission.[124] At the same time, it revealed how the understanding of the unity of the church also acquired accentuations that it thus far had lacked on the whole. The unity of the church and the struggle for it was not to be a matter of how the churches "deal with their own internal conflicts," as the document puts it,[125] but to include that struggle in the world's search for reconciliation, renewal, and humanity's unity and thereby make it relevant "in view of the immediate crisis of our time."

> In the agonizing arena of contemporary history — and very often among the members of the Churches — we see the work of demonic forces that battle against the rights and liberties of man, but we also see the activity of the life-giving Spirit of God. We have come to view this world of men as the place where God is already at work to make all things new, and where he summons us to work with him. The engagement in such work enables us to see fresh implications in the oneness, the holiness, the catholicity and the apostolicity which in close interdependence have always characterized the authentic life of the Church.[126]

Again it is especially the concept of the "catholicity of the church" which becomes the leitmotif, a kind of corollary of the "unity of the church." It intends the "deeper, inner dimension" of

124. Uppsala, 27-36.
125. Uppsala, 12.
126. Uppsala, 12.

unity, "the fullness, the integrity, and the totality of life in Christ," which "is the opposite of all kinds of egoism and particularism."[127]

"Catholicity" as a gift of the Spirit to the church at the same time points beyond the church to the "unity of humankind." For the same life-giving and renewing Spirit of God who bestows catholicity on the church is also at work in the world, and the church must participate in this work.

Thus the "gift" of catholicity bestowed on the church is at the same time "a task, a call, and a commitment" for the church. As the Holy Spirit bestows this catholicity on the church, it "empowers the Church in her unity to be a ferment in society, for the renewal and unity of mankind."[128] Not only in its own ranks but everywhere in the world must the church, therefore, oppose human division, discrimination, degradation, and exploitation as a "denial of catholicity." In this sense, "the Church is bold in speaking of itself as the sign of the coming unity of mankind."[129]

This emphatic orientation of the understanding of unity beyond the unity of the church and toward the *reconciliation and the unity of human beings,* as expressed at the Assembly of Uppsala, is seen also at the same time in confessional world conferences and in what they declare about the unity of the church, for example, the Lambeth Conference (1968) or the Assembly of the Lutheran World Federation (1970).[130]

This perspective on the understanding of unity has endured since then. Even though it is utterly wrong to think that it was absent from the earlier ecumenical movement, it can be said now that this perspective is strongly present everywhere in ecumenical efforts today. The understanding of unity has taken on a new form and has expanded as a result of that perspective.

This is also true in bilateral and multilateral ecumenical dialogues that intentionally and specifically endeavor to establish unity among churches, communion in the apostolic faith, in the sacra-

127. Uppsala, 13.

128. Uppsala, 14.

129. Uppsala, 17.

130. "The Renewal of the Church in Unity," section III in The Lambeth Conference 1968, *Resolutions and Reports,* 119–22. Study Document for the Assembly of the Lutheran World Federation in Evian (1970) with the title "More than Unity of the Churches" (*LR* 1 [1970]: 43-44).

ments, and in ministry. Despite the concentrated effort to overcome questions of faith and of church order that still stand between churches, it is accepted that, properly understood, the unity of the churches in faith, sacraments, and ministry cannot be pursued as merely an end in itself and apart from the mission of the church. It would be erroneous to do so simply because faith, sacraments, and ministry are themselves already tied to that mission.[131]

Problems in Determining the Aim of Ecumenicity

The justification and importance of the impulses of Uppsala for the understanding of the church's unity and the endeavor of ecumenism notwithstanding, they have since then also brought about a profound *uncertainty* in relation to the aim of the ecumenical movement. This weighs heavily on the movement. The Uppsala Assembly itself signals this in its reference to those voices that question "the basis of our effort for unity" and assert that "the struggle for Christian unity in its present form is irrelevant in light of the immediate crisis of our time," because in that struggle the churches are preoccupied only with "regulating their own internal conflicts."[132]

This view may perhaps have provided a very opportune foundation for the emphatic stress on the mission aspect, but it also indicated a renewed *juxtaposition of two forms of ecumenical effort,* a juxtaposition that was already present in the initial phase of the ecumenical movement. It had been overcome in its structural respect, however, by integrating it into the World Council of Churches itself and into the understanding of unity in the declaration of New Delhi.

Today these two forms of ecumenical endeavor and of the aims of ecumenicity appear again and again. They are present, on the one hand, in the dialogues between churches and their search for consensus and, on the other, in the "conciliar process for justice, peace, and the integrity of creation" that seeks commitment to common

131. This cannot and need not be elaborated in reference to the dialogues. It may suffice to recall the Lima declaration (1982) with its consistent reference to the ethical and social implications of baptism, Eucharist, and ministry.

132. Uppsala, 12.

action (see below 3.3.4.). The manner in which these two forms manifest themselves today, however, is much like the constellation they formed in the twenties and thirties, in the side by side existence of the "Faith and Order" and the "Life and Work" movements and in their confrontations.

When asked, people today insist that both forms of ecumenical endeavor basically *belong together,* of course. This togetherness remains questionable and endangered, however, as long as it is not supported by the understanding of why and in what manner those two forms are and must be *correlated* in terms of their substance and essence and not merely from the perspective of their immediate relevance and urgency for life. It would appear, however, that to date sufficient and common agreement is still lacking on this point.

Since Uppsala right up to the present, the consequence of this has been repeated polarization between an *"ecumenism of consensus"* focused on the churches, as it is often described, and an ecumenism of common action focused on the world and the problems of our age. In the seventies the latter was sometimes called *"secular ecumenism,"* and it is now usually identified with the "conciliar process for justice, peace, and the integrity of creation."[133]

133. Recent popular ecumenical discussion has applied the more radical concept of an ecumenical "paradigm shift" to this new or changed emphasis in the understanding of unity. The thesis developed by Konrad Raiser in his *Ecumenism in Transition: A Paradigm Shift in the Ecumenical Movement?* (Geneva: WCC, 1991) is related to this phenomenon only indirectly. His presentation is certainly permeated by the critique of "ecclesiocentric" ecumenical thinking and acting. He even goes as far as saying that the "ecclesiological orientation" is the "central element of the paradigm (up to now)" (71). But he is concerned with much more than that. Otherwise, he would not be able to include in "the old paradigm" (52) the Uppsala understanding of unity and its emphatic orientation beyond the church and its unity. Raiser's concern is the entire paradigm as it was up to now; he characterizes it in terms of Visser 't Hooft's concept of "Christocentric universalism." For Raiser, the "concentration on the church and its unity" is only one result of that paradigm or, as he puts it, a "direct consequence of the belief in the universal significance of the Christ event" (71). He thinks that this belief or the ecumenical paradigm it has shaped reaches its limits as the result of "the qualitatively new challenges of the present situation" (126 in the German original, deleted from the English translation) and is now being replaced by a new and emerging paradigm. Its place is being taken by what he thinks should be called a "trinitarian" paradigm. It is, however, a paradigm that speaks of the second person of the Trinity only in a highly untrini-

In light of this, the ongoing importance of the New Delhi declaration is apparent once again.

It describes the visible sought-after unity of the church in such a way that the dimension of mission — the "common life, which reaches out in witness and service to all," and the "common action . . . to the tasks to which God calls his people" — belongs insolubly to that unity itself. Apart from this, one cannot speak of the visible unity of the church.[134] In view of the present world situation, it is precisely this aspect that has acquired urgency and importance. This is not reflected in fact in New Delhi, but it gives a special character to the present understanding of the unity of the church and the struggle for it.

Yet the understanding of the church's unity must not be so restricted to this aspect — neither in the determination of the fundamental aim nor in the concrete praxis of ecumenical endeavor — that other aspects are pushed aside as irrelevant. The unity of the church has, indeed, other dimensions that are just as inseparably part of it, so that neglecting them would equally deny visible unity of the church.

This is precisely what the declaration of unity of New Delhi refers us to. It is a summary and condensation of the biblical and universal Christian understanding of the unity of the church. Even necessary reassessments of the understanding of unity must, therefore, not abandon the framework put in place by the declaration.

---

tarian way, namely, in the form of a "concrete Christology" (91), a Christology "from below" (62), one that speaks of "the historical figure of Jesus and his praxis" (78). But this is far removed from the accepted bases of the ecumenical movement; one need only recall the basis of the WCC and its confession of Jesus Christ as "Lord . . . , God and Savior." It is not necessary to devote more than a footnote to this matter. Raiser himself speaks repeatedly of the "hypothetical" character of language about a new paradigm (32–33), of an "assumption" that has yet to be verified (54), and refers to the still open question of its "reception" (127 in the German original, deleted from the English translation).

134. The conclusion of the report of New Delhi (New Delhi, 133) states: "In this concern for unity at every level of church life, we are mindful that the unity we seek is not for its own sake nor even for our sake. It is for our Lord's sake and for that of the world which he died to save." This reflects a conviction that the ecumenical movement has held from its beginnings.

2.3.2.4. The Unity of the Church as "Koinonia" (Communion)

In recent years, the understanding of the unity of the church has undergone a particularly important revision through a new consciousness of the New Testament and early church understanding of "koinonia/communio." The retention of the Greek or Latin concept for "communion" shows that a return to the thought of the New Testament and early church is intentional.

It is important to note that this consciousness of the koinonia/communio concept is not simply a matter of stressing and developing only one detailed aspect in the understanding of unity, comparable to what was discussed above as reassessments of the understanding of unity. Now it is rather a question of the understanding of church unity as a whole, indeed, the understanding of the church as such.

The Emergence of the Idea of Koinonia

It is quite true that the koinonia/communio concept in this sense had its place in ecumenical thought from the beginning of the ecumenical movement, at least as far as its content is concerned. This could not be otherwise in view of the fact that the apostolic confession of faith describes the "holy Christian (catholic) church" as a *"communio (sanctorum)."*[135]

As we have already indicated, however, only at the World Council of Churches' Assembly in New Delhi does this concept move more strongly into the center of the understanding of unity. Its full meaning was not obvious, however, for the universal ecclesiological renaissance of the concept of koinonia/communio was still in its beginnings.

Only in the course of the 1980s did koinonia/communio become an explicit, widely accepted leitmotif in the ecumenical movement. This occurred first in the bilateral dialogues and especially

135. Cf. especially the World Conference for Faith and Order in Edinburgh, 1937. See Edinburgh, 236ff.; also Lausanne, 463; and later Evanston, 85.

where they were concerned with the question of the understanding of the church.[136]

This shows that the koinonia/communio concept was and is, first and foremost, not a specifically ecumenical but an ecclesiological concept. It owes its special emphasis to the new developments of ecclesiology, which at the time of New Delhi were still not very visible and determinative. It is a question of ecclesio-

136. This can clearly be shown. In the World Council of Churches, especially in the Commission on Faith and Order, the concept koinonia/communio increasingly became a theme only in the years after the Lima declaration (1982), despite all that had already been stated at New Delhi. At the World Council of Churches Assembly in Nairobi (1975), there was indeed a "definition" of the unity of the church that contains the essential aspects of koinonia, but the concept itself was not used (Nairobi, 60). At the World Council Assembly at Vancouver (1983), the concept was still lacking, even though the ideas developed there — "eucharistic vision" of the unity of the church — come close to it. The decisive date in this connection is the Assembly of the World Council of Churches in Canberra (1991) with its declaration, "The Unity of the Church as Koinonia: Gift and Calling" (Canberra, 172-74).

It is more in the bilateral dialogues on the world level that the koinonia/communio concept is used and taken up as a theme — but as an ecclesiological concept. The first clear, albeit brief, references are found in 1976 in the Moscow declaration of the Anglican-Orthodox dialogue (No. 24) (41–49), then in 1977 in the report of the Reformed-Roman Catholic dialogue (Nos. 54 and 56) (434–63). In the first phase of the Anglican-Roman Catholic dialogue (ARCIC I) the concept is found in the narrower meaning of "koinonia of the churches" in reference to the "koinonia of local churches." See *Authority in the Church I, 1976,* No. 23 (97); *Elucidations from 1981,* Nos. 6 and 8 (103–4). The interpretation given in the introduction to the final report, composed in 1981, namely, that for "all our statements . . . the concept of koinonia has been fundamental" (No. 4) (64) cannot be verified, at least not terminologically. Nevertheless, this introduction from 1981 is the first instance of a more detailed use of the koinonia/communio concept in the area of bilateral dialogues (Nos. 4–9). In the same year (1981) the report of the dialogue between the Disciples and the Roman Catholic Church also speaks in some paragraphs of the church as koinonia/communio (Nos. 58–61). From this point on, the use of the concept intensifies in the bilateral dialogues, especially where the subject is ecclesiology. The Munich declaration of the Orthodox-Roman Catholic dialogue (1982), concerning the "Mystery of the Church and of the Eucharist in the Light of the Mystery of the Holy Trinity," is the first great example which is followed by others. Many of the references to dialogue materials can be found in Harding Meyer and Lukas Vischer, eds., *Growth in Agreement: Reports and Agreed Statements of Ecumenical Conversations at the World Level* (New York: Ramsey, 1984). (The page numbers in parentheses above indicate the texts that appear in the English edition of *Growth in Agreement.*)

logical developments especially in the Orthodox churches ("eucharistic ecclesiology") and the Roman Catholic Church ("communion ecclesiology") before and during the Second Vatican Council but particularly in the course of its reception. On the Protestant and especially the Lutheran side, the koinonia/communio concept emerged since the 1950s ever more strongly from ecclesiological concerns and from there moved to ecumenical concerns, where it gave greater depth to concepts like "altar and pulpit fellowship" and "church fellowship" that had long been in use.[137]

The Contribution of the Idea of Koinonia to the Understanding of Unity

What does the ecclesiological concept of koinonia/communio yield for the understanding of unity? And what makes it so attractive ecumenically?

The first thing to note is that it does not add aspects to the understanding of unity, as portrayed in New Delhi and in its reassessments, that were not already present. The declaration of the Assembly of the World Council of Churches in Canberra (1991) — "The Unity of the Church as Koinonia: Gift and Calling" — shows this. In its central part it states:

> The unity of the church to which we are called is a koinonia given and expressed in the common confession of the apostolic faith; a common sacramental life entered by the one baptism and celebrated together in one eucharistic fellowship; a common life in which members and ministries are mutually recognized and reconciled; a common mission witnessing to the gospel of God's grace to all people and serving the whole of creation. The goal of the search for full communion is realized when all churches are able to recognize in one another the one, holy, catholic, and apostolic church in its fullness. This full communion will be expressed on the local and the universal levels through conciliar forms of life and action. In such communion churches are bound in all aspects of their life to-

137. See, e.g., the volume *Koinonia. Arbeiten des Ökumenischen Ausschusses der VELKD zur Frage der Kirchen- und Abendmahlsgemeinschaft* (Berlin: 1957).

gether at all levels in confessing the one faith and engaging in worship and witness, deliberation and action.[138]

The continuity, indeed extreme congruence, with the formula of unity of New Delhi is apparent. Thus the koinonia/communio concept, in its application to the unity of the church, represents no "new" vision of the ecumenical goal. It does not lead away from the understanding of unity present up to now, and it does not lead beyond it.

a. Deepening and Bringing Alive the Understanding of Unity

This concept, however, does indeed lead more deeply into the understanding of unity by disclosing the unity of the church from within, that is, from the nature of the church. The koinonia concept is, indeed, well suited for this not least because it is closely related to the great New Testament images of the church, such as the trinitarian images of "people of God," "body of Christ," and "temple of the Holy Spirit."

Congruent with the confession of the *"communio sanctorum,"* the ecclesiological concept of koinonia signifies in the first place a more *elementary* understanding of the church that, to a certain extent, makes that understanding *more alive* and *concrete.*

Church is a lived "communion" of human beings and grows and lives from the fact that human beings have "communion" with the triune God, who lives in the "communion" of the three persons — as Father, Son, and Holy Spirit — and turns to humankind.

Thus in every respect church is "life in relation" — whether viewed "from above" or "from below," in its "vertical" or in its "horizontal" dimensions.[139] And the kind or quality of this relation — whether in the relation of human beings to one another, whether in their relation to the triune God, or in the relation among three divine persons — is always "communion" as understood in the specific meaning of the New Testament concept of

138. Canberra, 173.

139. Thomas F. Best and Günther Gassman, eds., *On the Way to Fuller Koinonia: Official Report of the Fifth World Conference on Faith and Order* (Geneva: World Council of Churches, 1993), 231. (In the following cited as Santiago de Compostela.)

"koinonia": participation, giving or receiving a place, and sharing with one another. Therefore, at its core meaning, koinonia is *"our shared life."*[140]

> "Koinonia" . . . describes the richness of our life together in Christ: community, communion, sharing, participation, solidarity.[141]

b. The Integrative Power of the Idea of Koinonia

This fundamental understanding of the church, completely informed by the koinonia concept, opens up a perspective in which the question of and search for the unity of the church insert themselves directly. The different dimensions and aspects as well as the reassessments of the understanding of unity also directly find their place and become recognizably clearer in their ordering and coherence. The koinonia/communio understanding of the church thus shows a decidedly integrative power for ecumenical thought.

The concept of koinonia has been accorded a high degree of acceptance in current ecumenical thinking and has become a key concept and guiding principle because it has given the understanding of the church a more elementary and more alive dimension and because it possesses an integrative power in relation to the understanding of and the struggle for the church's unity.

This should be explained briefly in at least its most important points.

1. Whatever has always been said and must still be said about "unity" as an essential attribute of the church and, therefore, about the necessity of efforts for the unity of the church is already stated in the designation of the church as koinonia/communio — *per definitionem.* The concept "koinonia," or "communion," does not require such an attribute as "unity"; it carries it within itself. For a "communion" that is divided or includes division within it stands in contradiction to itself.

The koinonia concept is thus in its allocation to the church a categorical connection of *church and its unity.*

140. Santiago de Compostela, 231.

141. Santiago de Compostela, 225. (The message of the conference.)

2. If church is understood as a "community of human beings" in the sense of the koinonia concept, which is to say, as a community of participation, of taking and being given a place, and of sharing, then what has been and must be said about the necessary "visibility" of the unity of the church, its concreteness, its being lived and experienced is already included in the concept of church. Of course, it has to be developed but does not first have to be explained.

The koinonia concept thus anchors the church and its unity from the start in the area of visibility, the ability to be experienced, and corporeality. And so it gives direct evidence of the reference and demand of *"visible unity."*

3. When the understanding of the church as koinonia is taken with complete seriousness, no sociological or ethical superficiality of the church and its unity occurs. The church then cannot be understood merely as a human merger, however deep the feeling of solidarity and important the common ethical concern may be that motivate such a merger. The church as "communion of human beings" arises and lives from the communion with the triune God, which is given to human beings in faith.

The center of koinonia, therefore, is the *communion in faith* and that which wakens and strengthens this common faith: the preaching of the gospel in common worship and in the common celebration of the sacraments.

4. At the same time, it is a special characteristic of the New Testament concept of koinonia that it makes directly apparent how faith and action are connected and how the centrality of faith is never allowed to be understood as if it impaired in some way the commitment to active service for others. From the koinonia with God, bestowed by God through faith on human beings, in which God is there for them and in which they themselves "take part" in God, there arises among humankind a koinonia of the same sort and quality: a communion of presence one to another, of participation and sharing. Church as koinonia of human beings certainly lives *from* faith, but it also lives *in* active responsibility and *in* service one to the other, directed to the need of others or to the common need.

Thus *faith and ethical action* are connected in the understanding of the church as koinonia. Both are connected in an indissoluble and, at the same time, irreversible ordering. This equally indissoluble and irreversible ordering of faith and action also applies, in light of the koinonia concept, to the understanding of church unity and for the ecumenical striving for communion in faith and in action.

5. In contrast to the concept "unity" which possesses a logical gradient to "homogeneity" and uniformity, the koinonia concept struggles from the outset against the thought of standardization. For communion lives and develops in relation to its "different" members. "Diversity" is, therefore, a constitutive element in the understanding of communion. Diversity is the very presupposition for the emergence of the relation of participation and sharing that constitutes the kind and quality of koinonia. In this sense, God's triunity is the paradigm of koinonia.

Thus, in the concept of koinonia, it becomes apparent how *diversity* and *unity* belong together in the church.

6. Structures and institutions belong to the visibility and concreteness that designate koinonia. They protect the communion in faith and make the one in action possible. Here the koinonia concept also has a watchdog function. Ecclesiastical and ecumenical structures and institutions must conform and be beneficial to koinonia: to koinonia as a "life in relation" and hence to the variety and diversity that belong to this life.

Therefore the *structural and institutional aspects* of the church and of its unity find their correct place in the koinonia concept.

7. Finally, the idea of koinonia moves the church and its unity onto the horizon of the *comprehensive act of God's salvation* in Christ for the reconciliation of the world with God himself (cf. 2 Cor. 5:19). "Reconciliation" and "communion" are in fact concepts that mutually interpret each other.

It can be said, therefore, with the World Council of Churches' Assembly in Canberra:

> The purpose of God according to holy scripture is to gather the whole of creation under the Lordship of Christ Jesus in whom, by the power of the Holy Spirit, all are brought into communion with God (Eph. 1). The church is the foretaste of this communion with God and with one another. The grace of our Lord Jesus Christ, the love of God, and the communion of the Holy Spirit enable the one church to live as sign of the reign of God and servant of the reconciliation with God, promised and provided for the whole creation. The purpose of the church is to unite people with Christ in the

power of the Spirit, to manifest communion in prayer and action, and thus to point to the fullness of communion with God, humanity, and the whole creation in the glory of the kingdom.[142]

All that has been said is only a very condensed and, to be sure, interpretative restatement — focused entirely on how unity is *understood* — of what has been said about "koinonia" as "the description of the church's visible unity" in recent years, particularly those between the Canberra Assembly in 1991 and the Faith and Order World Conference in Santiago de Compostela in 1993.[143]

All of this shows that the acceptance of the New Testament/early church concept of koinonia does not offer a formula that solves the ecumenical problem. It does show, however, that it integrates the understanding of unity, enlivening and deepening it to a high degree — all this on the condition that its meaning is not trivialized or used in a one-sided way.

At the same time, it gives expression to the fundamental continuity in the understanding of unity and with it the continuity in the determination of the ecumenical aim. Clearly, the concept of a "fully committed fellowship," which had been a key concept in the declaration of unity of New Delhi and which had integrated at that time different dimensions of the church's unity, occurs here again but in a deeper form.

2.3.3. A Look at Bilateral Dialogues

It must be noted that bilateral dialogues have hardly had an impact on the development and reassessment of the understanding of unity as such. Their effort was directed primarily at the discussion of the controversial questions between the churches. The question of the understanding of unity is not specifically addressed, with the exception of a document from the Catholic-Lutheran dialogue.[144] When statements about this subject occur, it is for the most part in the context of the

142. Canberra, 172. The World Conference on Faith and Order in Santiago de Compostela also makes this point again and again, e.g., 225–26.

143. Santiago de Compostela, 230.

144. "Ways to Community" (1980), in Meyer and Vischer, eds., *Growth in Agreement,* 215–40.

specific ecclesiological problematic. That is, it is a question of unity as one of the attributes of the church's essence.

What is stated in the dialogues on this topic is, on the one hand, determined by specifically confessional interpretations of the unity of the church, as outlined above (2.2.), and, on the other, remains in the framework of the understanding of unity as it has been shaped in the ecumenical movement and which was the subject of this entire chapter.

The latter aspect is demonstrated in a short and condensed paragraph from the document *Facing Unity* (1985) of the Catholic-Lutheran Dialogue Commission.[145] This paragraph about the nature of unity summarizes what the Commission had detailed in the previously mentioned document of 1980. It is placed alongside the New Delhi declaration of unity, to which — as is expressly stated — "it corresponds in essential aspects."[146]

> The unity of the church given in Christ and rooted in the Triune God is realized in our unity in the proclaimed word, the sacraments, and the ministry instituted by God and conferred through ordination. It is lived both in the unity of the faith to which we jointly witness, and which together we confess and teach, and in the unity of hope and love which leads us to unite in fully committed fellowship. Unity needs a visible outward form which is able to encompass the element of inner differentiation and spiritual diversity as well as the element of historical change and development. This is the unity of a fellowship which covers all times and places and is summoned to witness and serve the world.[147]

Real impulses for the understanding of unity came from the bilateral dialogues only when the concept of koinonia entered the discussion. In fact, it appears that the koinonia concept first arose in the bilateral dialogues and largely from there gained its importance

145. Joint Lutheran/Roman Catholic Study Commission on the Gospel and the Church, *Facing Unity: Models, Forms and Phases of Catholic-Lutheran Church Fellowship* (Geneva: World Council of Churches, 1985); the German text is *Einheit vor uns: Modelle, Formen und Phasen katholisch/lutherischer Kirchengemeinschaft* (Paderborn: Bonifatius-Druckerei, 1985).

146. Joint Lutheran/Roman Catholic, *Facing Unity,* 8.

147. Joint Lutheran/Roman Catholic, *Facing Unity,* 8.

for general ecumenical thought. This was indicated previously (see footnote 136).

To be sure, reference must once again be made to the fact that in bilateral dialogues the koinonia concept appears not as much as an ecumenical concept, that is, directed to the unity between churches and Christians, but primarily as an ecclesiological one, related to the nature of the church. It proves itself suitable in the dialogues for overcoming differences in the understanding of the church and showing what is held in common. The titles of those appropriate dialogue reports show that the koinonia concept is primarily a central ecclesiological concept in those dialogues: "The Church as Communion,"[148] "The Church as Communion in Christ,"[149] "The Church as Koinonia/Communio Founded in the Trinity,"[150] and other similar texts.[151]

To offer a description of what is said in these texts about the "church as koinonia" would go beyond the framework of this volume and its subject.[152]

148. "The Church as Communion," in *Report of the International Anglican/Roman Catholic Commission* (Rome: 1991).

149. "The Church as Communion in Christ," in *Report of the International Dialogue Commission between the Disciples of Christ and the Roman Catholic Church* (1994).

150. Chapter 3.3. and, in connection with it, chapter 3.4. of the Catholic-Lutheran dialogue document *Church and Justification: Understanding the Church in the Light of the Doctrine of Justification* (Geneva and Rome: 1994). The original German text is *Kirche und Rechtfertigung* (Frankfurt am Main: 1994).

151. The third dialogue between Pentecostal churches and the Roman Catholic Church, entitled "Perspectives of Koinonia" (1985–1989) (Rome: 1990), is also a dialogue about the church.

152. On this, there exist initial investigations; see, e.g., Susan Wood, "Ecclesial Koinonia in Ecumenical Dialogues," in *One in Christ* (1994/2): 124–45.

3. *Models of Union*

3.1. Understanding of Unity and Models of Union

Having looked at the question of how unity is understood, we now address the matter of how it is achieved. The issue now is the concrete formation of unity: union. A number of different forms or patterns of possible concretization of unity present themselves. One speaks of them as "models of union" (cf. 1.2.). "Models of union" are, therefore, operative transpositions of the understanding of unity.

3.1.1. The Necessary Correspondence between Models of Union and the Understanding of Unity

If models of union are operative transpositions of the understanding of unity, then the decisive issue about the development and assessment of these models is whether they correspond to the understanding of unity as it has been shaped in the ecumenical movement and informed it. One can speak of a "model of union" in the full sense, that is, as a form of the realization of visible unity of the church, only where this model of union is formed in such a way that it does justice to all the essential dimensions and all the constitutive elements of visible unity.

In relation to the understanding of unity as it has become determinative for the ecumenical movement (see above 2.3.), each model of union has to guarantee that in it a "fully committed fellowship" (koinonia) is realized and therefore must include:

- communion in the understanding and confession of the apostolic faith,
- communion in the sacraments,
- communion in ministry,
- communion in worship life,
- communion of action in witness and service in the world and the structured presuppositions required for it.

A model of union that lacks one of these dimensions or constitutive elements or that concentrates on only one of them while ignoring others can thus only be viewed as a model of *partial* union. It represents at best a level of realization of unity but cannot be regarded as a completely valid model of union.

The debates of the 1970s concerning models of union summarized this in four basic requirements, to which each model of unity must correspond and by which one determines whether it, in fact, signifies "the realization of true ecclesiastical unity" (see above 2.3.1.). At a consultation between representatives of the World Council of Churches and the Christian world communions in October, 1978, which referred to the results of the First Forum on Bilateral Dialogues and the meeting of the Commission on Faith and Order of the same year, it was stated:

> Agreements were reached in regard to concepts and models of unity, although not final and complete. These may allow us to go beyond this discussion and focus our attention on these four requirements for unity as defined in the Forum (on Bilateral Conversations): a) ending prejudices and hostilities and lifting condemnations; b) sharing one faith; c) being able mutually to recognize baptism, eucharist, and ministry; d) agreeing on ways of deciding and acting together. These requirements appear to us to be fundamental for every realization of true church unity, whatever model of union one is inclined to prefer in a given situation and on a given level of church life.[1]

1. The Relations Between the World Council of Churches and the World Confessional Families. *Consultation Report,* no. 9 (Geneva: 1978). Quoted by G. Gassmann and H. Meyer in "The Unity of the Church: Requirements and Structures," *LWF Report* 15 (June 1983): 50.

3.1.2. The Necessary Openness of the Understanding of Unity to Different Models of Union

Even if models of union — as operative transpositions of the understanding of unity — must correspond to the understanding of unity, it is certainly not the case that a specific understanding of unity works with or proposes only one specific model of union.

This is true of confession-specific understandings of unity as they were portrayed in the preceding pages. Indeed, they have, as will be demonstrated, clear affinities to specific models of union and are not compatible with every model. At the same time, however, different models of union can be represented for one and the same church or confessional family, or conversely one and the same model can be affirmed in different churches and confessional families.

This is also true in relation to the understanding of unity as it has been formed in the ecumenical movement. On the basis of the understanding of unity from New Delhi and its reassessments, models of union could and still can be developed and represented which are different one from the other and still — for the most part, correctly — claim to be in line with the New Delhi understanding of unity.

This shows that the understanding of unity prejudices, to a certain degree, the question of the model of union. In this respect the understanding of unity has, without a doubt, a basic delimiting function, but at the same time it offers within this framework a considerable, albeit limited, openness for different models of union.

It is not a weakness of the understanding of unity, for example, in the sense of a lack of precision, that one and the same understanding of unity is able to be realized operatively in different ways and hence be open to different models of unity. On the contrary! Rather this proves that in different situations, for different churches and ecclesiastical traditions and different levels of church life, this understanding of unity is operatively realizable and quite capable of conferring a common orientation on the ecumenical struggle taking place in different circumstances.

The openness of the understanding of unity to different models of union thus means its openness to necessary, contextually determined concretizations and to its validity for different situations and conditions in and under which the struggle for unity takes place.

The insight that *different models* of union can exist, which are nevertheless operative transpositions of *a common understanding of* unity, that is to say, the differentiation between understanding of unity and models of union, is relatively new.[2] It is extremely important, however, for the cohesion and progress of the ecumenical movement. It certainly does not relieve us of the question of which model of union is appropriate between specific ecclesiastical partners and in a specific situation. It does, however, remove from the dispute about models of union — a dispute that has permeated the ecumenical movement from its beginning — the narrowness and sharpness that have often characterized it.

Common understanding of unity and *different* models of union: that too is a necessary application of the principle of "unity and diversity" to the ecumenical effort itself. And it is very significant that this important insight really begins to assert itself in that time when the positive evaluation of diversity generally began to gain acceptance in the ecumenical movement (see 2.3.2.1.).[3]

The context in which this comes about is again the debate of the 1970s about the models of union, which will be discussed later (see 3.3.1. and 3.3.1.4.). One of the central questions of that time was whether — in line with the predominant conception in the ecumenical movement until then — ultimately only one legitimate model of union could exist, namely, the model of "organic union" or whether other models such as that of "unity in reconciled diversity" were also possible. The result of the debate was that not just one of the two models of union but both could be the full realization of the visible unity of the church. The Commission on Faith and Order stated at that time (1978):

> The two concepts are not to be seen as alternatives. They may be two different ways of reacting to the ecumenical necessities and possibilities of different situations and of different church traditions.[4]

2. Statements on the distinction between "unity" and "union" had already been given, but they had not been accepted. Cf. G. Gassmann, *Konzeptionen der Einheit in der Bewegung für Glauben und Kirchenverfassung 1910–1937* (Göttingen: Vandenhoeck and Ruprecht, 1979), e.g., 27, 66, 69.

3. It was occasionally formulated in the discussions that there was not only variety and diversity "in" unity but also "of" unity, i.e., of the realization of unity.

4. Bangalore (1978), Geneva (1978), 240.

The principle of "common understanding of unity — different models of unity" was expressed even more clearly at a consultation during the same year in Geneva, which has been quoted already (see above 3.1.1.):

> Whether a "realization of true ecclesiastical unity" exists is decided on the basis whether it corresponds to the understanding of unity, i.e., the "four basic requirements" of ecclesiastic unity, "regardless of the question, of preference to a particular model of unity in a specific situation and on a specific ecclesiastical level."

3.1.3. Special Factors in the Determination of Models of Union

The reason that the one, common understanding of unity is and must be open to diverse forms of realizing unity is that in the concrete formation of ecclesiastical unity other factors in addition to the understanding of the church's unity alone come into play. Models of union, indeed, have to correspond to the understanding of unity, but they are not simply derivable from it. Rather — as always with the passage from conception to concretization — *situation-conditioned factors* come into play.

The statements of the Faith and Order Commission and the Geneva consultation of 1978 cited above make mention of this when they speak of the different "situations," "ecclesiastical traditions," and "ecclesiastical levels" that codetermine the question of the models of union:

- Churches with distinctive consciousness of their historical heritage and their confessional particularity will develop or choose models of union in which confessional identities are not surrendered or blurred but can be preserved as legitimate diversities.
- Churches in which consensus in doctrine is of special importance for their life and their own cohesion will strive for a realization of unity in which the explicit consensus of doctrine is given particular weight.
- Other churches again will ascribe, for analogous reasons, special priority in the concrete embodiment of unity to common fea-

tures in worship and liturgy or to common features in ministry and ecclesiastical structures.

- Where in the life and thought of Christians the mission motive emerges strongly, there will be a requirement or a preference for models of union in which the aspect of common mission in witness and service is determinative.
- Likewise the *"situation"* — religious, social, cultural, spiritual, and economic — in which Christians and churches live constantly proves to be a codeterminative in the concrete realization of ecclesiastical unity.
- Where Christians and churches are clearly in the minority vis-à-vis other religions and experience this situation as a missionary challenge or as a threat to their existence, the ecumenical effort focuses — as is constantly demonstrated — on models of union with the greatest possible inner and structural unity, which protects the ecclesiastical existence and strengthens the missionary action.
- Where the situation of their country or continent especially challenges Christians and churches to give priority to effort for the poor and against social injustice in their life and action, forms of ecclesiastical unity that promote solidarity in this effort will be sought.
- Ecclesiastical traditions and traditional confessional heritage that have historically developed in western Christianity and can demonstrate there their continuing value for the unity of the church are perceived by Christians in other areas as foreign and, therefore, as a burden to the realization of ecclesiastical unity.
- In the context of a society that understands itself as pluralistic and has consolidated itself as such, it is more obvious and plausible to pursue analogous ecclesiastical models of union than in one where the building of the state and society (nation building) is still in process and must assert itself against the dividing powers of existing differences.

It is obvious that what are frequently referred to as *"levels of ecclesiastical life"* can also codetermine the manner in which unity is realized. The realization of unity on a worldwide level, that is, between geographically widely separated churches, will proceed differently in many respects than between Christians and churches in one and the same country or in one and the same city or local community. It is true, the closer Christians and churches live beside one another and the more they share the same concrete life situation, the closer and more concrete is the realized and lived out unity that is formed.

All these varied models of union that result from these and similar factors, however, are "realizations of true ecclesiastical unity" as long as they remain within the framework of the common understanding of unity, that is to say, as long as they fulfill not only some but all the basic requirements of church unity and thus include the constitutive elements of unity. This common understanding of unity remains the criterion of the different models of union.

3.2. Basic Positions — Basic Models

In the course of the first decades of the ecumenical movement, *three basic positions* regarding the question of the concrete realization of ecclesiastical unity emerged. These positions are still recognizable today. They can be spoken of as the basic "models of union," but one must remember that the important distinction between the understanding of unity and models of union, as they became popular after New Delhi and especially in the 1970s, was still not worked out then in a clear fashion.[5] Both the understanding of unity and models of union were still closely interwoven. The possibility that, on the basis of a common understanding of unity, there can be different but fundamentally legitimate forms of realization, having equal weight, was still not sufficiently recognized. Whether a correct understanding of unity was present became clear, therefore, in terms of the specific model of unity that was supported. This, at least, was the clearly predominant tendency. Until recently this often gave the debate on models of union, however important that debate is, a sharpness and narrowness that it should not have.

The development of these three basic models has been de-

5. Reference to Gassmann (see footnote 2 in this chapter) and what he says about the distinction between "unity" and "union" (esp. 27, 66, 69).

scribed in detail.[6] They are clearly outlined in the years between the first World Conference for Faith and Order (Lausanne, 1927) and the second World Conference (Edinburgh, 1937). The Edinburgh Conference describes these basic models under the heading "The Different Concepts of Church Unity" and designates the first model as "cooperative action" or confederation, alliance, federation, the second as "intercommunion," and the third as "corporate union" or "organic union."[7]

Since then it is common to speak of these three models, for the most part, as *"federation," "intercommunion,"* and *"organic union."*

Behind these concepts and their meaning exists a longer history as well as debates and differences of opinion that are clearly rooted in different and in part specific confessional ecclesiologies. The boundaries between the models are not always clear, the usage of words not always unambiguous. Thus there is an awareness that the exact definition of the three models is difficult. This cannot be described more exactly here.[8]

At the World Conference in Edinburgh the description of the three models is connected at the same time with an evaluation.

- In an absolutely unambiguous manner the conference sees in "organic union" the proper and complete realization of unity: it is the "final aim of our movement," "the ideal."[9]
- In contrast, "federation" is "not our final aim"; it is, at best, a step, a "way to a more complete form of unity."[10]
- Regarding "intercommunion," a detailed judgment is lacking, but it is clear that it too is not valued as a complete realization of unity but only as "a necessary part of any satisfactory Church unity."[11]

When the historical background and wider context of the discussions and reflections of that time are examined, the question

6. In particular the study by Gassmann should be mentioned in this connection.

7. Edinburgh, 250–53.

8. The account by Gassmann gives the best insight.

9. Edinburgh, 252.

10. Edinburgh, 251.

11. Edinburgh, 251.

arises whether the unambiguous option for "organic union" and the derogatory judgment of the other models have not had a negative impact on the objective evaluation of the last two models. It would appear that favoring the decision for one of the models caused the description of the others to be foreshortened, thus, legitimating the favored decision in advance.

Since the issue now is not primarily the view of the Edinburgh World Conference but rather the description of the three basic positions in as neutral and thorough a manner as possible, the views presented prior and during the conference are to be considered as much as possible in the following reflection. We can, therefore, follow the sequence of Edinburgh itself without adopting the evaluation made there.

3.2.1. The "Cooperative-Federal Model"

History

This model of ecclesiastical union was accessible to the ecumenical movement for a long time. It goes back into American Protestantism of the nineteenth century, which was strongly characterized by the Great Awakening. Names that come to mind particularly are those of the American Presbyterian and subsequent founder of the Disciples of Christ, Thomas Campbell, and his document "Declaration and Address" (1809) and the Lutheran Samuel S. Schmucker, a pioneer of the "Federal Council of the Churches of Christ in America" (founded in 1908) and his "Fraternal Appeal to the American Churches" of 1838.[12]

The notion of a cooperative-federal union strongly determined the Movement for International Friendship and the Life and Work Movement, 1910–1925.[13] It was also especially represented by many on the Protestant side within the movement of Faith and Order, for example, at the first World Conference in Lausanne (1927).

12. Cf., e.g., Gassmann, *Konzeptionen,* 34–42.

13. Cf. Ruth Rouse and Stephen Charles Neill, eds., *A History of the Ecumenical Movement, 1517–1948* (Philadelphia: Westminster, 1967), 509–42.

This first model of union that the Edinburgh Conference describes is designated as "cooperative action."

> The unity which we seek may be conceived of as a confederation or alliance of Churches for cooperative action.
>
> In all areas where common purposes and tasks exist, such action is already widely possible without violation of conscience. Church "federations" are the most common expressions of such unity, and one of the most hopeful paths to understanding and brotherly relations. We believe federation, so construed, is a promising approach to more complete forms of unity. . . .
>
> We recognize that federations for cooperative action should not be construed as examples of "federal union. . . ."
>
> We are agreed that cooperative action between Churches unable to achieve intercommunion or to look towards corporate union, and compelled by fidelity to conscience to remain separate bodies with separate loyalties, is not our final goal, since cooperative action in itself fails to manifest to the world the true character of the Church as one community of faith and worship as well as of service.[14]

Form and Characteristics

This model has two characteristics:

First, Edinburgh reiterates throughout that the heart of the matter is the *common action* of Christians and churches, their "cooperative action." It is, in particular, their common action in evangelization/mission and their joint humanitarian and social service.

This communion of action cannot just exist at certain points and be limited to specific areas of action but must be comprehensive. It is not an option, nor can it be terminated at any time. It is obligatory, not only occasionally, now and then, but must have the element of duration. Therefore, this commonality of action of Christians and churches must accept firm forms. For the present, it is a secondary matter whether it is a question of how the "federation" is organized or of some other firm form or structure. The conviction that marks this model is important: the unity of the church must be-

14. Edinburgh, 250–51.

come visible primarily in the common, that is, comprehensive, committed, and permanent action of Christians and churches.

Second, this communion of action can become effective within the *continuing independence of the churches,* not only in their legal form but also in their special features of confession. However this communion may and must find structural form, these structures are of such a kind that they do not impair or cancel but rather preserve and protect the liturgical, theological-confessional, and constitutional uniqueness and identity of the individual churches. Here is the second typical characteristic of this basic model, and the concepts "federation" or "federal" refer to it.

> . . . the related Churches remain clearly distinct from one another in their own eyes and in the eyes of those who look at them from without. They still function as separate bodies. Their individual history can still be written.[15]

Insufficient or Sufficient Model of Union? Critique and Defense

The big question that arises in view of this first basic model is whether and how it lacks constitutive elements of ecclesiastical unity, indeed, must lack by definition on the basis of those two determining characteristics. The cooperative-federal union would then be, in fact, not a completely valid basic model of ecclesiastical unity. It would be a certainly representative but, in light of the understanding of church unity, not a defensible model of unity. This is the question to be addressed not only in historical retrospection but also in basic ecumenical reflection. Therefore, it must be examined here.

As already stated, this is the critique of the Edinburgh Conference. It declares: For the cooperative-federal form of ecclesiastical unity there is no need for "likeness in faith or confession," no "likeness in nonsacramental worship," no "likeness in doctrine and administration of the sacraments," no "likeness in ministry," and no "likeness in order." For, as it is constantly stated, all this is "*not neces-*

15. Thus the preparatory document for this area of the question: *The Meanings of Unity* from the pen of Angus Dun (New York: Harper and Brothers, 1937), 35; Edinburgh, 251.

sary for cooperative action."[16] As a result, this form of unity could not be deemed a complete realization of ecclesiastical unity.

If these statements are correct, if a cooperative-federal realization of unity ignores and can ignore especially communion in faith and confession, worship, sacraments, and the church's ministry, then the judgment of the Edinburgh Conference is correct.

Neither in historical retrospect nor from objective consideration, however, is it possible to be satisfied and accede to this portrayal and judgment. On the whole, the cooperative-federal model was by no means presented in such a one-sided, narrow, and undifferentiated fashion.

Yet such voices were indeed heard; in a "bewildering variety of forms,"[17] much of what presented itself as organized Christian, ecclesiastical cooperation (Bible societies, missionary councils and societies, etc.) often also pointed in that way. Rightly or wrongly, the Life and Work Movement was also perceived in this way.[18] The perceptions of this model, however, especially as it was represented by the non-Anglican communities, had a much greater depth than the constricted representation of Edinburgh reveals.[19]

Structurally formed, practical cooperation, that is to say, an "instrumental" understanding of unity — as it was referred to at that time — clearly prevailed.[20] Primary interest was focused on this understanding. Yet it was not a question only and exclusively of cooperative action, so that other elements and aspects of unity that were more strongly related to the churches themselves were excluded as unnecessary.

This is already evident in the Lausanne World Conference, especially in its Section VII, where the central issue was "what final form the church should have according to God's will."[21] The work in this section was so heavily burdened by sharp tensions between the representatives of organic union and those of the cooperative-federal action form of unity that the section report could not be adopted in common but only presented to the churches for further discussion.

16. Edinburgh, 252–57. It is here that the three models are compared with one another.

17. Dun, *The Meanings,* 29.

18. Dun, *The Meanings,* 34.

19. Cf. Gassmann, *Konzeptionen,* 83ff.

20. Dun, *The Meanings,* 27.

21. Cf. Lausanne, 435–37.

Nevertheless, the divergence of the concepts was not as wide as the portrayal by Edinburgh seemed to suggest. Otherwise, how would the other section reports about the gospel, the nature of the church, the common confession of the faith, the church's ministry, the sacraments have been accepted "unanimously"? That is why the report of this Section VII was also opened and then pervaded by common statements of both groups about the necessity of unity in faith and the necessity of the church's ministry and of the sacraments for the church. As it is stated, "there is a common agreement that, in the final analysis, 'Life and Work' and 'Faith and Order' need one another if they wish to reach their goal."[22]

This certainly did not cancel the tension between the representatives of those two models of unity — neither in Lausanne nor in the subsequent period. It allowed recognition, however, that the representatives of the cooperative-federal concept did not exclusively restrict themselves to cooperative action so that everything else would appear to them as "unnecessary" for unity. Many among them did not deny the necessity of communion in confession, in the sacraments, and in ministry, but what they advocated was the idea of a "federation with full eucharistic and pulpit communion."[23]

What emerged here among the advocates of the federation concept and what they explicitly supported was a form of achieving unity that did actually contain the two specific characteristics of the cooperative-federal model: specific orientation toward commonality in action (practical cooperation), on the one hand, and preservation of ecclesiastical independence and confessional uniqueness, on the other. But at the same time, that form integrated the constitutive elements of church unity. Already in Lausanne such a concept had expressly been named as one of three concepts of "federation."[24] It is also described as "federal union."[25]

In view of this, it is quite odd and remarkable that following the

22. Cf. Lausanne, 435–36.

23. Thus Gassmann, *Konzeptionen,* esp. 179f. and 184.

24. Lausanne, 362–65, the remarks of Bishop Hognestad. See the German text of Lausanne, edited by Hermann Sasse (Berlin: 1929), 548, with a summary of conference discussion. "The word 'federation' is used with at least three meanings: 1. a substitution for organic union; 2. a step on the way to organic union; 3. a form of organic union."

25. Dun, *The Meanings,* 35; Edinburgh, 251 and 253.

Lausanne Conference and even at the Edinburgh Conference people resisted counting such a form of federation (i.e., the "federated union") as part of the cooperative-federal model and acknowledging that *in this form* the cooperative-federal model may, indeed, be a fully valid model of union. Rather the opposite was asserted, namely, that this was no longer the federation model,[26] a view that allowed the devaluation of the cooperative-federal model to continue as such and in general.

This was, as it has been justly said, a "severe shortcoming" of the Edinburgh Conference, "which gives rise to the suspicion that in the interest of a disposition, leading to corporate union, this form of unity has been consciously excluded as a possible goal."[27]

In fact, it must be asked whether the way in which Edinburgh portrayed the cooperative-federal model does not approach the "caricature" about which the preparatory document for the Edinburgh Conference had expressed a warning.[28]

In brief, the description and evaluation provided by Edinburgh of the cooperative-federal model of union, which have caused this model to be widely devalued, require critical scrutiny. The extent to which the cooperative-federal model of union can be delivered from the shadow of its Edinburgh evaluation will permit it to be seen as a genuine "basic model" of union and be supported. Otherwise, it does, indeed, signal only a partial union or one step on the way, however important such preliminary forms of church union may be.

26. Dun, *The Meanings,* 33; Edinburgh, 251.

27. Gassmann, *Konzeptionen,* 270.

28. The preparatory document, "The Meanings of Unity" (cf. note 15 in this chapter), represents matters in a more differentiated way than does Edinburgh itself. It states that it is a "caricature" when "the advocates of organic union depict federation in such a way that it is no unity at all but merely a very loose association of existing churches" (42). Gassmann believes that there is a "more positive" assessment of federation in Edinburgh (*Konzeptionen,* 179, 269f.). His use of the comparative is correct. Prior to the conference there were indeed voices to be heard, particularly in the Anglican communion, that rejected federation outright as a "denial of the visible unity of the church." (Dun, *The Meanings,* 43f. ". . . I hate it [the federal system] and think it is impossible," said Anglican theologian A. S. Duncan Jones; Gassmann, *Konzeptionen,* 259f.). In comparison, Edinburgh is indeed "more positive," inasmuch as federation is seen to be a "promising way toward more complete forms of unity" (Edinburgh, 251). Yet cooperative-federal union is no complete form of unity and, for that reason, cannot be "our final goal" (251).

Problems and Challenges

The preceding references have made it clear that the Edinburgh portrayal and evaluation will have to be questioned in historic perspective. This is also basically true, however, in relation to the assessment of the model of cooperative-federal union itself. It is not appropriate to reduce this model as such and in every form to a mere preliminary form of ecclesiastical union. Rather, it is that this model possesses an inner ambivalence. Whether it is a completely valid model or only a preliminary form of ecclesiastical union depends finally on itself, or more exactly, it depends on its two basic characteristics, its "cooperative" orientation and its "federal" form. At the same time, it is ultimately a matter of two closely connected questions that address the alternatives.

First, does the "cooperative" aspect of this model of union, that is, its *primary orientation toward the common action* of the churches, imply and intend the renunciation of the struggle for communion of the churches in confession of faith, in sacraments, worship, and ministry? Or is the effort for "interecclesiastical" communion, for its realization and its serious theological confirmation in regard to this communion, included as necessary?[29]

Second, does the "federal" form of this model of union, that is, the *continuing independence and uniqueness of the churches,* mean that as far as the relation of churches one with another is concerned, there is no desire for a closer interecclesiastical communion, and the present side-by-side existence of churches should be left as it is? Or is this form of union proposed out of the desire to protect differences that are acknowledged to be legitimate and in this way conform to the nature of ecclesiastical communion?

29. The first question undoubtedly touches the weak point of a striving for unity oriented primarily toward commonality of action (cf. above 2.3.2.3.). The same conclusion emerges in considering the early discussion about the cooperative-federal model of union (cf. Gassmann, *Konzeptionen,* 90f., 294f.). The weakness lies in the tendency to devalue the questions about faith, doctrine, and even order that arise among churches, in order to advance the interest of common action directed toward the world and, having devalued those questions, regard the efforts to answer them as superfluous. What is overlooked is that the churches' common action needs to be anchored in the churches' communion in order to be truly encompassing, binding, and lasting.

Whether the cooperative-federal model represents only a preliminary form or a completely valid basic model of church union that corresponds to the understanding of unity is decided in terms of these two questions.

Thus to defend the cooperative-federal model of union is simultaneously a call to this model and its advocates not to lose sight of the communion in faith, worship, and ministry that is necessary for the church's unity in the justified pursuit of commonality in action and not to back away from efforts to achieve that communion.

Now there are, without doubt, many and diverse cooperative-federal unions, which, in fact, are only "preliminary forms" of ecclesiastical unity and understand themselves as such. Their ecumenical significance is beyond question. One need only think of the national Christian councils and the working study groups of Christian churches or the World Council of Churches, which justly regard themselves as preliminary forms of ecclesiastical union.

In no way, however, does this mean that such unions are, and must always remain, mere preliminary forms of ecclesiastical union on account of their cooperative orientation and federal forms. If and as soon as they correspond to the understanding of unity and its criteria, they are, regardless of their cooperative orientation and federal form, complete realizations of ecclesiastical unity.

There are also examples of this, such as the "confessional world alliances," which understand themselves as realizations in the full sense of ecclesiastical unity among their member churches, their federal structures and strongly cooperative pursuits notwithstanding. As a result they have described themselves correctly for some time as "communions" in the full sense of the koinonia/communio concept.[30] Conversely, there exist more recent organic union formations that are characterized by a clearly cooperative-federal nature yet are not denied recognition as full realizations of church unity.[31]

30. Since 1980 the collective concept is "Christian World Communions." A concrete example is the Lutheran World Federation, which is designated as "federation" and is structured as such; in its present constitution, however, it is understood as a "communion."

31. The "Église du Christ au Zaire" is such a case.

3.2.2. The "Model of Mutual Recognition"

History

This model of ecclesiastical union is clearly the most recent of the three basic models. Even though the ecumenical use of the concept of recognition is quite old, only in the period between the Lausanne and Edinburgh Conferences did "mutual recognition" appear as a determinative idea of an independent model, in clear distinction to the other two.[32] Nevertheless, the contours of this model were still blurred. One could say that this model profiled itself completely only in more recent times, namely, in the concept of "church fellowship" as it was developed in the 1950s especially in the Reformation churches and its application experienced in the Leuenberg Agreement (1973) (see 3.3.1.2.).[33]

The Edinburgh Conference itself does, indeed, present this second basic model in its report as a special model of union, but it also strangely obscures its full form.[34] One must, for this reason, go beyond the report of the Edinburgh Conference to get a complete view of this form of ecclesiastical union.

The report of the conference designates this model of union with the term "intercommunion" and says:

> A second aspect of Church unity is commonly indicated by the term "intercommunion." This is the fullest expression of a mutual recognition between two or more Churches. Such recognition is also manifested in the exchange of membership and ministrations.
>
> We regard sacramental intercommunion as a necessary part of any satisfactory Church unity. Such intercommunion, as between two or more churches, implies that all concerned are true Churches, or true branches of the one Church.[35]

32. Dun, *The Meanings,* 17–26.

33. The view of "unity in reconciled diversity" (1974) is historically and objectively related closely to the concept of "church fellowship" (in German *"Kirchengemeinschaft"*). (See 3.1.3.)

34. Cf. the concluding observations of the research by Gassmann in *Konzeptionen,* 296f.

35. Edinburgh, 251. The following two paragraphs speak of different forms or gradations of intercommunion (full intercommunion, open communion, communion at conferences, as they were later and more accurately defined at the Faith and Order Con-

Form and Characteristics

The designation of this model of union as "intercommunion" without a doubt notes something important, even central, but it is inadequate as a full description of this model of union.

It is true that eucharistic communion among churches, in the sense of the thought and practice of the ancient church, is possible only if there are no differences among them that divide the church and if it is obvious, therefore, that the churches together are part of the one church of Christ. Ecclesiastical unity finds in intercommunion the "fullest expression" (Edinburgh) and intercommunion, as it were, seals ecclesiastical unity.[36]

Nevertheless, as the Edinburgh Conference correctly says, communion in the Lord's Supper is only "one side," "a necessary part" of ecclesiastical unity. Other "sides," "parts," or aspects must be present where it is a question of the unity of the church and its realization.

This is clearly understood in Edinburgh when in speaking about the model of "intercommunion" it refers in its report also to the "exchange of membership and ministrations." It is clearer still when, comparing the three models of union in detail, it is shown that "likeness in faith or in confession," in "worship," in "doctrine and the administration of the sacraments," and in the "ministries" are part of "intercommunion."[37]

This second model of unity thus comprises more than communion in the Lord's Supper. It should be named differently in order to avoid a narrowing of the model through the *pars-pro-toto* designation "intercommunion." The concept used in Edinburgh, "mutual recognition," offers itself as an appropriate designation, to be completed by the addition Edinburgh made, namely, recognition as "true Churches, or true branches of the one Church."

In fact, the preparatory document for the Edinburgh Conference — *The Meanings of Unity* — had designated and described more comprehensively and correctly this model of union in the sense of *"unity*

---

ference in Lund [1950] and in the Faith and Order document, *Beyond Intercommunion: On the Way to Communion in the Eucharist,* 1971; see footnote 135 in ch. 2).

36. "Complete fellowship in the Church will not be realized until the way is open for all God's children to join in communion at the Lord's table." Lausanne, 437.

37. Edinburgh, 253–57.

of mutual recognition."[38] Only in this way does it become clear that what is encountered here is really a complete and independent model of ecclesiastical union.

In naming the typical characteristics of this model of union, three characteristics must be highlighted.

First, in contrast to the cooperative-federal model and its primary concerns, the focus of this model of union is the *relation of the churches to one another,* that is, the unity *ad intra.* The task is to examine, chiefly in dialogue among churches, what differences have divided them — in faith and doctrine, sacramental life, and ministries — with the aim not necessarily to resolve and remove the differences but rather to deprive them of their church-dividing component. Another aspect of the primary concern at work here is to achieve the recognition and acknowledgment of the churches and their diversities as legitimate expressions of what it is to be church, as "true Churches, or true branches of the one Church" (Edinburgh).

Second, at the same time the unity of "mutual recognition" — and here there is a closeness to the cooperative-federal model — can be realized with the *continuing institutional independence* of the churches and their confessional uniqueness or identity intact, provided that this confessional uniqueness or identity is proven in the process of common examination to be legitimate. "They (the churches) remain in view of their management quite separate governmentally and are in the same measure distinct bodies, as they were previously."[39]

Third, both identified characteristics show that for the model of mutual recognition the *problematic of unity and diversity* is particularly determinative. Within the framework of this model, it requires such an intensive and differentiated treatment as is true with no other model. The model of mutual recognition thus finds its place "between" the tendency to renounce the examination and clarification of existing differences between the churches in favor of cooper-

38. "Unity of mutual recognition" (Dun, *The Meanings,* 17–26). "Intercommunion" appears here only as one of three aspects of this model.

39. Dun, *The Meanings,* 26. This becomes clear on the basis of the intercommunion of the Church of England with the Church of Sweden or with the Old Catholic Church. "Intercommunion," it is thought, changes nothing in the independence and uniqueness of the churches. It has "an almost completely declaratory character."

ation and coexistence as it is found, at least occasionally, in the cooperative-federal model, on the one hand, and the tendency to eliminate or cancel the existing differences and peculiarities in general, as the model of organic union demonstrates it, on the other.

Even though we must still discuss possible deficits and reductions of the model of mutual recognition, we may say already that this model of union corresponds to the understanding of unity and thus represents a fully valid model of ecclesiastical unity. The Edinburgh Conference report, especially the part which compares the three models with each other, makes this apparent as well.[40] Clearly, where the churches recognize one another as "true Churches, or true branches of the one Church" there is nothing which still separates these churches for the sake of faith and conscience.

Both the Edinburgh Conference and its preparatory document express certain reservations about the model of recognition. Ultimately, the reason for this is their declared option for only one of the models, namely, that of organic union. It alone appears to embody the ecumenical "ultimate aim" or "ideal"[41] inasmuch as this model of union allows currently existing churches to cease being "distinct and separate bodies," each with its own identity. This shows that the necessary distinction between understanding of unity and models of unity (see 3.1.2.) is not sufficiently recognized in Edinburgh. Only one model of union — allegedly — can correspond to the understanding of unity, and every other model of union is at best a preliminary form or a step on the road toward unity.

Problems and Challenges

But even the plea for the model of recognition as a full and independent model of church union must meet certain conditions. Three aspects are involved.

First, the legitimate interest in the relation of the churches to one another, which characterizes this model of union, must not lead to a repression or impairing of the aspect of mission; for this aspect belongs to the understanding of unity (see above 2.3.2.3.)

40. Edinburgh, 250–53.
41. Edinburgh, 251–52.

to which each model of union must correspond if it is to be regarded as completely valid. Here may be a temptation inherent in the recognition model, one that is to be opposed. The communion of the churches among one another seeks expression also in the commonality of action in witness and service for the world.

Second, the question of common structures is closely connected with this. The model of mutual recognition of the churches must not be misunderstood or misused in the sense of a mere juxtaposition, a mere coexistence of churches. The communion of the churches requires common structures if it is to be effective in the life and action of the churches. It concerns once again the issue that the model of union must correspond to the understanding of unity (see 2.3.2.2.). To be sure, the structures of communion must be of the kind that respect and protect the legitimate difference of the churches.

Finally, the model of recognition has often been reproached for sanctioning the *status quo* of the churches and leaving everything as it was. However, this is an imputation. It conceals the fact that the transition from a situation where churches set themselves apart from and judge one another to one where they mutually accept and recognize one another means a radical change in ecclesiastical self-understanding. And such a change in self-understanding cannot occur without a redefining of existing traditional and confessional positions.[42] Nevertheless, that reproach can be a warning cry. Mutual recognition of the churches cannot be viewed as the "easiest" form of the ecumenical movement that allows the churches to move closer to the unity sought without, so to say, making a move.

42. It is interesting to see that where the concept of "mutual recognition" appears in ecumenical documents for the first time, it is immediately connected with the necessary "transformation of the churches." "Whichever way leads to the goal, complete unity presupposes that the churches be so transformed that the members of all church communions are in a relation of full mutual recognition" (see Lausanne, 436–37).

3.2.3. The "Model of Organic Union"

History

The idea and concept of "organic unity" derive from Anglican thought.[43] It is to be noted that the predicates "organic" and "corporate" mean materially the same. They appear for the first time in the same context in which the Chicago-Lambeth Quadrilateral (see 2.2.2.) arose and are closely connected to it: the American Protestant Episcopal Church of the 1870s and 1880s and in particular one of its theologians, W. R. Huntington.

Like the Quadrilateral, the idea of organic unity or union was received in all of Anglicanism and determined the statements of the first three Lambeth Conferences (1888, 1897, 1908) on the unity of the church.

If one considers how closely the emergence of the Faith and Order Movement is connected with the Protestant Episcopal Church in North America and its ecumenical initiatives, it is not surprising that we encounter the idea and concept of "organic unity" already at the beginnings of the Faith and Order Movement. Already in 1913, in the joint theses of the preconference for the planned world conference, "organic unity" is stressed as the "ideal" "that all Christians should pursue in their thought and prayer."[44]

The first world conference itself (Lausanne, 1927) certainly did not speak in this way. The tensions at the conference between the Anglican advocates of this model of union and the predominantly Protestant representatives of the "cooperative-federal model" were too great. The subsequent world conference (Edinburgh, 1937) first speaks of organic union as the ideal realization of the final ecumenical aim.[45]

This idea prevailed from that time on within the Faith and Order Movement and essentially also in the World Council of Churches into the 1970s.

In the report of the Edinburgh Conference we read the following under the title of "corporate union":

43. See Gassmann, *Konzeptionen,* 15–34 (footnote 2 in this chapter).
44. Cf. Gassmann, *Konzeptionen,* 80f.
45. Edinburgh, 252–53.

> The third form in which the final goal of our movement may be expressed presents, from the standpoint of definition, the greatest difficulties. It is commonly indicated by such terms as "corporate union" or "organic unity." These terms are forbidding to many, as suggesting the idea of a compact governmental union involving rigid uniformity. We do not so understand them, and none of us desires such uniformity. On the contrary, what we desire is the unity of a living organism with the diversity characteristic of the members of a healthy body.
>
> The idea of "corporate union" must remain for the vast majority of Christians their ideal. In a church so united the ultimate loyalty of every member would be given to the whole body and not to any part of it. Its members would freely move from one part to another and find every privilege of membership open to them. The sacraments would be the sacraments of the whole body. The ministry would be accepted by all as a ministry of the whole body.
>
> Our task is to find in God, to receive from God His gift, a unity which can take up and preserve in one beloved community all the varied spiritual gifts which He has given us in our separations. . . .
>
> While we do not conceive of the "corporate union," which we seek from God, as a rigid governmental unity, we find it difficult to imagine that unity as it would exist between Churches within the same territory without some measure of organizational union. At the same time, we can hardly imagine a corporate union which would provide for the relative autonomy of the several constituent parts in entire neglect of the "federal" principle.
>
> In particular . . . we do not believe that a Church "corporately" united could be an effective international community without some permanent organ of conference and council, whatever might be the authority and powers of that organ.[46]

Form and Characteristics

There can be no doubt that organic union, as it is described here and more extensively explained in the subsequent conference report,[47] represents — in the light of the understanding of unity considered

46. Edinburgh, 252–53.
47. Edinburgh, 252ff.

— a fully valid model of union. Since the conference itself puts very great and exclusive emphasis on this model, it needs no additional advocacy as in the case of the first two models. The Edinburgh text is itself an eloquent advocacy, especially as regards the tone and substance of apologetic and supporting elements, substantiations and differentiations that are part of such an advocacy.

What are the distinguishing characteristics of this model of ecclesiastical union? Four interrelated characteristics are to be noted.

First, like mutual recognition, organic union also has to design anew the *relation between the churches* and to overcome the existing divisions between them. Just as mutual recognition, organic union also requires "likeness in faith or confession," which is a "necessary requirement." It also requires likeness in worship, in "nonsacramental worship" but also and directly in the sacraments, their understanding (doctrine), and their administration. It is necessary here to reconcile the "differences between the churches." The same is true for the offices (ministries), their differences in conception, and their form.[48]

At the same time, it is not a question here of "rigid uniformity." Diversities are permissible. The communion, as it states, "(can) comprise and preserve all the different spiritual gifts, which we have received in our separated communities from him (i.e., God)."[49]

To be sure, much points to the fact that organic union demands "a high degree of likeness in the norms of belief, in the types of common worship, in the use of sacraments, in the forms of ministry, and in polity."[50] In comparison with the model of mutual recognition, the relation of unity and diversity is seen entirely within the horizon of the idea of organism and gains a more strongly harmonizing character from it. Yet this leads already to the second dominating characteristic of the model of organic union.

Second, as in the model of mutual recognition, one might think at first glance that the issue was, first and foremost, a matter of the relation of different churches "one to another." In reality, however, the issue is clearly more extensive. Diversities are comprehended and bound together in an institutional and constitutional ecclesias-

48. Edinburgh, 254–57.
49. All this follows from a comparison of models (esp. Edinburgh, 252–59).
50. Edinburgh, 252–53.

tical unity that hinders, indeed forbids, the institutional embodiment of diversities, that is, in the form of independent churches or ecclesial communities. This means that from the relation of churches "one to another" a relation of "in one another" arises so that in the strict sense one may speak of *"one church."* It is exactly this, and nothing less, that the idea and concept of "organic" or "corporate" intends.[51]

In contrast to both the cooperative-federal and the mutual-recognition models, the model of organic union strictly rules out the possibility of institutionally independent churches with special — including confessional — form and identity within the accomplished unity. This is the real pathos of this model. When hitherto divided churches that live "in the same territory" enter into organic union, they cease to exist as institutionally identifiable entities. What comes into being is a single church with its own new identity. The undivided loyalty of its members belongs to this single church and no longer to the churches from which they came and from which the union has been formed.

> Corporate church union . . . takes place when independent and self-determining religious bodies form one body where there were two or more previously. In terms we have used, it occurs when Churches that have behaved as two bodies begin to behave as one body.[52]

> In a church so united the ultimate loyalty of every member would be given to the whole body and not to any part of it.[53]

Third, *the unity of governmental union* belongs to organic union, in which the different churches become "one church," "one" corpo-

51. This concept is directed not only against a purely "functional" or "instrumental" unity, i.e., one oriented to common action. It is directed even more against the intent to preserve institutionally legitimate ecclesiastical diversities, as this is expressed in the federal model and in the model of recognition.

52. Dun, *The Meanings,* 39. Previously it was stated there: "The most general objective work of Corporate Unity is behaving as a body, functioning as a living whole, maintaining recognizable identity in space and time" (36). However, "In the Unity of Mutual Recognition and the Unity of Cooperative Action, as we have sought to describe them, the related Churches remain clearly distinct. . . . They still function as separate bodies. Their individual histories can still be written" (35).

53. Edinburgh, 252.

rate body. This also distinguishes the union model from the other two models in which the churches "in their governance remain quite separate governmentally."[54] This concept of governmental unity or governmental union is found already in Huntington's preliminary form of the Quadrilateral.[55] It appears then as an important concept in the preparatory document for the Edinburgh Conference, where corporate union is described,[56] and in the conference report itself. Even though it is stated there that corporate union is not perceived as rigid governmental unity,[57] "governmental unity" does essentially belong to it. It is an expression and instrument of the institutional unity of the united church and guarantees that the united churches really "behave as a body" and "function as a living whole."[58] The "organic" thus really includes the "organizational."

> We find it difficult to imagine that unity as it would exist between Churches within the same territory without some measure of organizational union.[59]

Fourth, "unity of church government" cannot be thought of apart from the ministry of the church. Here too organic union demands a higher measure of commonality than the other models of union demand. It requires not just the mutual recognition of ministries but *"a ministry* acknowledged as *possessing the authority of the whole body."*

> By "a ministry acknowledged as possessing the authority of the whole body" is meant something more than likeness in the form of the ministry, or even a mutual recognition of ministries. It means that the ministry would be, in its inner meaning and outer action, an organ of the one body. That would certainly constitute an important aspect of what we have called Corporate Unity.[60]

54. Dun, *The Meanings,* 26.

55. The fourth point speaks of the "episcopate as the keystone of Governmental Unity" (see Gassmann, *Konzeptionen,* 17).

56. Dun, *The Meanings,* 37, 39, 41.

57. Edinburgh, 251. Here too the notion of "compact governmental union" was turned down (253).

58. Dun, *The Meanings,* 36f.

59. Dun, *The Meanings,* 36f.

60. Dun, *The Meanings,* 42.

Concerning this form of ministry, it would not be quite justified to say that it is a question here of the historic office of bishop. Without a doubt, this applies to Anglican thought, as is shown in the Quadrilateral and also in the Edinburgh report when it states that for some churches "the historic episcopate is essential for corporate union." It appears, however, that fundamentally the question of the form of this required office (ministry) for corporate union remains open.

This model of corporate union, described in these four characteristics, rests on specific presuppositions.

First, there stands in the background an understanding of the church for which the New Testament picture of the church as "body" — interpreted in the strictest sense of the word — is determinative. Within the body, there certainly are different members, but they are connected to a unified organism, and as such a unified organism the church intends to, and must, appear.[61]

Further, the reference to the church of the first centuries plays a considerable role. Envisaged is an indeed highly idealized picture of the early, undivided church, portrayed as the one communion of local churches, completely united and led by a single bishop.

Finally, the model of corporate union is marked to a high degree by the notion of the territorial-national church. Church is realized in the first place on the level of regional "territories," countries, or nations. The outer limits of a specific church are given through the limits of these "territories," and within these "territories" there should be only one church. The model of corporate union, therefore, applies in the first place, if not even exclusively, to the "territorial," that is, regional/national level of ecclesiastical life.[62] Beyond this, including at the international level, it applies only in considerably modified form.

61. Edinburgh, 252–53; see Dun, *The Meanings,* 41.

62. Edinburgh, 253: ". . . Unity, as it would exist between Churches within the same territory. . . ." Cf. also *The Meanings,* which repeatedly mentions "territorial churches" (38) or "territorial branches" of the denominations (35, 37) and where the specific examples of corporately united churches are always referred to national churches. Gassmann says that it is a question here of the "classical Anglican concept of united national churches" (*Konzeptionen,* 272).

Problems and Challenges

Before, during, but also after the Edinburgh Conference, all four characteristics of corporate union are so strongly emphasized that to the advocates of organic union every model of union that preserved traditional ecclesiastical-confessional structures appeared at best as a preliminary form of church union, if not even as a "negation of the visible unity of the church."[63]

It was pointed out repeatedly, especially by supporters of the model of recognition, that this exclusive claim of the model of union implied the basic devaluation of ecclesiastical-confessional traditions and diversities. This reproach is justified inasmuch as it refers to the tendency in the model of union to see ecclesiastical-confessional structures as one-sided and inclusively under the category of "sinful divisions."

The real problem of this model of union, however, ultimately lies in its exclusive claim. Despite repeated critique, the claim was maintained for decades. Hand in hand with the actual and long-lived predominance of this model in the Faith and Order Movement and the WCC as well, this claim has aggravated the churches' search for other forms of church union that correspond to their own self-understanding and unique situation as well as to the understanding of unity.

The predominance of the model of corporate union no longer exists today. At the latest, the discussion of the 1970s and the insight that different models of unity could correspond to the common understanding of unity have ended the exclusive claim of the model of union. This had been sensed in a vague way right at the outset but could not yet prevail.[64] The validity of the model of organic union, however, is not affected by this insight. Those who favor another model of union also acknowledge this model to a large extent.

63. Cf. Dun, *The Meanings,* 44.

64. Dun, *The Meanings,* viif. It states by way of introduction: "To examine the meanings of unity is not to prejudge the question as to whether there is some single formula which will define the unity to be sought in all places and circumstances." This thought comes close to statements of the Faith and Order Commission and in the Geneva consultation forty years later (1978). (See 3.1.2.)

3.2.4. Summary

1. It has been shown that already in the course of the first three decades of the ecumenical movement three clearly different models of ecclesiastical union emerged.

2. From an unprejudiced description of them, the conclusion can be drawn that, in light of the understanding of unity, each model can be viewed in principle as a completely valid form of the realization of ecclesiastical unity. The differences between the models of union are not radical and, therefore, also not in conflict. The common understanding of unity holds them together.

3. The real reason for the diversity of these models of union is that each is determined by a specific primary interest or concern, or, indeed, by a specific pathos, that stamps each model as a whole:

- the interest in the common action of the different churches that is directed toward the world (cooperative-federal model);
- the interest in the continuing value of the special ecclesiastical or confessional heritage of the different churches and in its maintenance in the realized unity (model of mutual recognition);
- the interest in the reuniting of hitherto divided churches of a region or country into institutionally unified territorial churches or — in this sense — "local churches" (model of corporate union).

4. In the light of the respective primary interest, there are various ways to address the question of "unity and diversity" and to use the ecumenical principle that "unity does not mean uniformity."

5. The character of the models stamped by their respective primary interest can but must not — measured in terms of the understanding of unity — lead to curtailment and one-sidedness. These dangers must be recognized and opposed.

6. The following applies in general terms: The insight that diverse models of union may correspond to the understanding of unity and that the choice of a model of union depends on the self-understanding of churches and their situation was too little developed in the early period and subsequently. This is the reason why the relation of the models of union one to another is seen all too quickly as one of conflict.

3.3. Ecumenical Processes

Developments and Advances in the Models of Union

3.3.1. The Debate about Models of Union 1973–1978

Common Presuppositions and Initial Phase of the Debate

Only in the 1970s was there once again an intensive debate about the models of union. It developed within the context of a considerable change in the overall ecumenical situation that was characterized in particular by two factors.

For one, at the Assembly of the World Council of Churches in New Delhi (1961), the understanding of the church's unity and of the aim of the ecumenical movement had been explained and articulated in their basic outline. This was done in such a way that the understanding of unity not only allowed for a single model of union but was also fundamentally open to other models (see 2.3.1.).

For another, the ecumenical movement had been considerably enlarged. There had been not only a quantitative enlargement but also a certain qualitative shift. The Orthodox churches had entered the World Council of Churches almost in their totality and were present at the New Delhi Assembly. At the Second Vatican Council, the Roman Catholic Church had embraced the ecumenical movement and become one of its important supporters. In both cases, churches that were stamped by a strong consciousness of their identity or confessionality entered onto the ecumenical agenda.

This again triggered a strengthened ecumenical engagement among the other confessional world alliances or worldwide Christian fellowships. Even though they had constantly affirmed and promoted the ecumenical engagement of their member churches — for example, their membership and cooperation in the World Council of Churches — they themselves had hardly been ecumenically active until then.

All of this soon resulted in a very large and ever-increasing number of bilateral dialogues between churches on the international and national level. These dialogues developed almost entirely outside of the World Council of Churches, since for this council — at least at that time — the multilateral form of ecumenical meetings and conversations was the basic priority.

Both presuppositions were in great measure influential in the new debate on models of union.

Though the debate on the models of union had abated since Edinburgh, specific developments had taken place within the period leading up to the new debate. They can be related to the basic models of ecclesiastical union as have already been described. It is especially a question of two lines of development. The first, that of "union formation or discussion about union," is clearly related to the model of corporate union and is, to a certain extent, the history of its concrete application. The second, that of the development and, ultimately, the application of the idea of "church fellowship," is more conceptual in nature and connected most closely to the model of mutual recognition.

3.3.1.1. Union Formations and Union Negotiations

In view of the explicit option of the Edinburgh World Conference for the model of corporate union, it is understandable that the Commission on Faith and Order of the World Council of Churches welcomed especially all endeavors for the formation of such ecclesiastical unions, advising and supporting them in various ways. Organic union remains here the "ideal," and the New Delhi declaration of unity (see above 2.3.1.) pointed at that time at least in this direction for those who drafted it.

Such church unions corresponding to, or aiming for, this ideal soon took shape. The first such union,[65] one regularly presented as exemplary, is the unification of Congregational Churches, the Methodist Church, and the Presbyterian Church in Canada, resulting in the "United Church of Canada." This happened in 1925, prior to the World Conferences of Lausanne and Edinburgh. Similar unions fol-

65. The World Council of Churches does not count the unions formed in nineteenth-century Germany among church unions, nor does the historiography of ecumenism. (E.g., cf. the large chapter on church unions in *A History of the Ecumenical Movement,* ed. Rouse and Neill, vol. I, 286–305; see footnote 13 in this chapter.) This is mentioned now only as a fact even though one would need to determine the reasons for that view. Presumably, the reasons are historical, that is, the primary preoccupation was with church unions that emerged from the ecumenical movement of the twentieth century.

lowed, for example, in China ("The Church of Christ in China," 1927), in Japan ("Church of Christ in Japan [Kyodan]," 1941), in South India (1947; today "Church of Christ in South India"), in the Philippines (1929/1948; "United Church of Christ"), in Pakistan ("Church of Pakistan," 1970), in Northern India (1970), in the Congo (1970, today: "Church of Christ in Zaire"). At the same time, numerous union negotiations occurred, especially in Africa and Asia but also in Great Britain.[66] The most extensive union negotiations since 1962 were — and are — in the United States: the "Consultation on Church Union (COCU)."

The at first glance very impressive number of unions and union negotiations is considerably reduced when inner-confessional unions and negotiations are eliminated and only the transconfessional, that is, ecumenically relevant unions and union negotiations are included.[67]

In regard to the previous confessional affiliation of the united churches, Reformed, Methodist, and Congregational churches are at the top of the list. On the other hand, Lutheran and also Anglican churches, in spite of their traditional approval of this model of union, have demonstrated a definite reserve.[68]

The establishments and negotiations of unions were accompanied by further reflection about the nature of "organic union." That reflection remains clearly within the framework of what was stated in the initial period and what was described above about this basic

66. Concerning the history of the ecumenical movement see Rouse and Neill, eds., *A History of the Ecumenical Movement,* vol. I, 286–304; for the period until 1970, see R. Groscurth, ed., *Kirchenunionen und Kirchengemeinschaft* (Frankfurt: O. Lembeck, 1971), esp. 99–114. In the *Ecumenical Review,* "A Survey of Union Negotiations" appears every two years. The most recent survey covers the years 1988–1991 (*ER,* vol. 44, 1992/1, 131–55).

67. In 1970, the year directly prior to the new debate, there were fifty-seven unions and thirty-one ongoing negotiations of which only twenty-three or, by some counts, nineteen have a transconfessional character (Groscurth, *Kirchenunionen,* 99–114). The *Dictionary of the Ecumenical Movement* (Geneva: World Council of Churches, 1991) speaks — strangely enough — of only eighteen transconfessional unions and fourteen transconfessional negotiations, but it states at the same time that according "to careful accounting about 20 million Christians belong to churches which understand themselves as transconfessional unions" (1,033f.).

68. See Groscurth, *Kirchenunionen,* 99–114, for the year 1970.

model of ecclesiastical union. Yet there were some new accentuations. These new accentuations can be detected in the report of the second consultation of representatives of union churches and those in union negotiations, which took place under the Commission on Faith and Order in Limuru (Kenya) in 1970, immediately before the new debate began. Under the heading "What is a united church?" six distinctive features that "most united churches reflect" were cited.

> A. They will be transconfessional and comprise churches that previously belonged to different confessional families.
>
> B. They will not only be united but uniting churches, conscious that they are not a terminus but a stage in the process of seeking full union in the Church.
>
> C. They feel themselves committed to manifesting the unity of the Church by gathering together all Christians in a given place.
>
> D. They are looking forward to the coming into existence of one united communion in all places.
>
> E. They seek to give theological expression to the gospel in the context of the present ecumenical movement and the contemporary world situation rather than in terms of inherited confessions.
>
> F. They have achieved organic unity in the sense that they are capable of making decisions as a united Church, in matters of faith and order, mission, outreach to the world, and the use of their own resources.[69]

The "new accentuations" in the understanding of organic union are seen especially in points A, B, D, and E and will be briefly commented on:

First, even more than in Edinburgh, organic union is clearly, yes, categorically marked by *"transconfessionality."* The Limuru Report itself states: ". . . church union is seen more and more in transconfessional terms."[70] "A union that does not expressly overcome the existence of one's own confession will lead to new breaks."[71] In the preceding period, this appears to have been stressed more and more strongly and was repeated in conjunction with a sharp criti-

69. The "Limuru Report" is found in *MidStream,* 9, no. 2–3 (1971): 4–32.
70. "Limuru Report," 32.
71. "Limuru Report," 13.

cism of the existence of "world confessional organizations" as the great hindrances of the ecumenical movement.[72]

The "conditions" of church union thus include a "new" and "common name," that is, the emergence of a new common identity and the "willingness to give up one's own (previous) identity."[73] Repeated reference is made in this sense to "dying and rising"[74] by way of allusion to the parable of the seed of wheat (John 12:24).

Second, the united churches consciously understand themselves as *"uniting* churches." This was and, in recent years, is stressed again and again and is addressed in points B, C, and D. It results from two facts: that as yet there is no church union that unites all Christians in a given place; and that united churches living in individual "places" need a comprehensive communion among one another, a "united communion in all places" as it is stated in point D.

Third, the communion in faith and confession that is constitutive for organic union, "the common fundamental position of faith"[75] or, as point E puts it, the sought-after "theological expression [of] the gospel," should orient itself more by the *"present world situation* than by the traditional categories of confession."

Fourth, a new accentuation is present in that it is now more apparent that *"different forms* of union" can exist "as they may result from cultural or other needs."[76] In addition, "the confessional background" of the churches uniting together and the "historical epochs" play a part. "Thus some united churches do not know an epis-

72. Well known and often quoted is the sharp criticism of world confessional associations by the East Asia Christian Conference in Bangalore (1961).

73. "Limuru Report," 13–14.

74. At issue here is a recurring theme in the description of organic union. For example, Stephen Charles Neill writes about corporate unions: "The final and terrible difficulty is that the Churches cannot unite unless they are willing to die. In a truly united Church there would be no more Anglicans, Lutherans, Presbyterians or Methodists. . . . Until Church union takes the shape as a better resurrection on the other side of death, the impulse towards it is likely to be weak and half-hearted. . . ." *A History of the Ecumenical Movement,* vol. I, 495. Cf. also G. F. Moede, "Church Union as a Model of Christian Unity" (Kirchenunionen als ein Model christlicher Einheit) in R. Groscurth, ed., *Wandernde Horizonte* (Frankfurt am Main: Lembeck, 1974), 92 and esp. 96f., also footnote 97.

75. "Limuru Report," in Groscurth, *Kirchenunionen,* 142.

76. "Limuru Report," in Groscurth, *Kirchenunionen,* 142.

copate; others have bishops, presbyters, and deacons."[77] The "Eglise du Christ au Congo" (known today as "au Zaire"), founded in the year of the Limuru Consultation (1970), is "a new model that grants to the uniting churches from the beginning a greater autonomy."[78]

Nevertheless, the claim that "organic union is the declared goal" basically survives. The consultation of Limuru "confirms this opinion. Each form of union falling short of this aim is unable to eliminate the aggravation of division."[79] Yet even then it seems that this claim could occasionally be retracted by the advocates of the model of union in its strict form, for instance, when it is said that the "unity given in Christ in the life of the church . . . can appear in different ways."[80]

Regarding terminology, one may say that the concept of "organic union" has more prominence than it had in Edinburgh and that the concept of "corporate unification" or "corporate union" recedes. This is important insofar as the latter concept becomes free, so to speak, to describe a different model of union (see 3.2.3.).

3.3.1.2. Idea and Model of "Church Fellowship"

History[81]

The conscious goal here is a different path and form of ecclesiastical unification than the formation of union. In substance, what is to be described now is clearly a further development and refinement of the

77. "Limuru Report," in Groscurth, *Kirchenunionen,* 150.

78. Moede, "Church Union," 19.

79. "Limuru Report," in Groscurth, *Kirchenunionen,* 141.

80. "Limuru Report," in Groscurth, *Kirchenunionen,* 141. This fluctuation between a claim which is maintained and revoked appears again three years later occasionally at the meeting of the Commission on Faith and Order in Salamanca (1973). There one can speak, on the one hand, of "church union" or "organic union" as "one of the expressions" of ecclesiastical unity but, on the other hand, of the "vision of conciliar fellowship" so that "it requires organic union" and can only be realized "if the churches are ready to face at every level the presuppositions and requirements of organic union." Groscurth, *Wandernde Horizonte,* 170f., and G. Gassmann, ed., *Documentary History,* 21 and 35.

81. On this point, cf. esp. H. Meyer, "Zur Entstehung und Bedeutung des Konzepts 'Kirchengemeinschaft,'" in *Communio Sanctorum. Einheit der Christen — Einheit der Kirche.* FS für Bischof Paul-Werner Scheele (Würzburg: Echter, 1988), 204–30.

model of mutual recognition that has already been discussed. This development and refinement occur within the churches of the Reformation. Reformation convictions about the church and its unity come into play here, such as Article 7 of the Augsburg Confession states them, or the quite similar statements of the Reformed church, such as Article 17 of the Second Helvetic Confession.[82]

The model of organic union is rooted in Anglicanism. In similar fashion, the model of church fellowship is grounded, as far as the history of its origins is concerned, in Reformation church thinking. Yet just as the model of union can be applied also outside the sphere of Anglicanism, the church fellowship model can find use not only among Reformation churches but also, with possible modifications, among other partners.

The use of the concept of church fellowship to designate a specific form of ecclesiastical unity apparently comes into play after the Second World War in connection with the transformation of the Protestant church of the Old Prussian Union into the Protestant Church of the Union (EKU). The reference there (1950) to the joined Lutheran, Reformed, and United communities as a "church fellowship" helps elucidate the meaning of that concept.

The concept is taken up by the Lutherans and deepened further theologically. Here the New Testament/patristic concept of "koinonia" plays an important role. Indeed, it appears as the equivalent of "church fellowship." Especially noteworthy here are the considerations of the Ecumenical Commission of the VELKD (United Evangelical Lutheran Church of Germany) and those of the closely associated Theological Commission of the Lutheran World Federation during the 1950s. The idea of church fellowship gains ever clearer contours here, and the term "church fellowship" becomes a programmatic, ecumenical concept. In view of the multitude of elements that belong to an ecclesiastical unity and which cannot be reduced to simple eucharistic fellowship, Peter Brunner proposed the term "church fellowship" *(Kirchengemeinschaft)* as incorporating all of these elements.[83] Some years later, the Lutheran World Federation

82. It is especially the last paragraph of this article to which reference is made.

83. Lutheran World Federation. Dept. of Theology, *The Unity of the Church: A Symposium. Papers Presented to the Commissions on Theology and Liturgy of the Lutheran World Federation* (Rock Island, Ill.: Augustana Press, 1957), 18.

could state the following about this concept: "The Lutheran churches participate in the ecumenical struggle of the present with a positive concept."[84]

Concerns and Characteristics

The concept and model of church fellowship show how churches differing in tradition or confessionality and hitherto separated are able to have full communion with one another without, as with organic union, having to surrender their confessional particularity, identity, or ecclesiastical independence.

Therein lies the specificity and special concern of this model of union, and for that reason it represents a refinement of the model of mutual recognition.

Behind this is a fundamentally positive evaluation of confessionality. The emergence of confessionally different churches did *in fact* lead to ecclesiastical divisions, yet their existence as confessionally different churches as such does not contradict the unity of the church. If the divisive sharpness and depth are removed from confessional differences, then these differences — of theological heritage, liturgical life, ecclesiastical order, and piety — become recognizably legitimate expressions of apostolic faith and of Christian and ecclesiastical life. As such, they have a continuing value and should, therefore, be preserved and treasured structurally and institutionally in the unity of the church.

The Example of the "Leuenberg Church Fellowship"

To date the clearest and most comprehensive application of this model of ecclesiastical union is found in the communion among Lutheran, Reformed, and United Protestant Churches in Europe. This church fellowship was explained and established by the Leuenberg Agreement of 1973. Important conceptual explanations in relation

84. The Nature of the Lutheran World Federation, no. 4, in Lutheran World Federation. Assembly (4th: 1963: Helsinki), *Document/Fourth Assembly of the Lutheran World Federation* (Geneva: The Lutheran World Federation, 1963), 19–20.

to the idea and model of church fellowship preceded it and are reflected in the text of the Leuenberg Agreement itself. Even though they are directed to the concrete case of Lutheran-Reformed relations, the relevant passages are probably the best description of this model to be found in ecumenical texts.[85]

> In the sense intended in this Agreement, church fellowship means that, on the basis of the consensus they have reached in their understanding of the gospel, churches with different confessional positions accord each other fellowship in word and sacrament, and strive for the fullest possible cooperation in witness and service to the world.

This is, as it were, a brief definition of "church fellowship." The following statements about the "Declaration of Church Fellowship," however, should also be included for a better understanding:

> In assenting to this Agreement the churches, in loyalty to the confessions of faith which bind them, or with due respect for their traditions, declare:
>
> a) that they are one in understanding the gospel as set out in Parts II and III;
>
> b) that, in accordance with what is said in Part III, the doctrinal condemnations expressed in the confessional documents no longer apply to the contemporary doctrinal position of the assenting churches;
>
> c) that they accord each other table and pulpit fellowship; this includes the mutual recognition of ordination and the freedom to provide for intercelebration.
>
> With these statements, church fellowship is declared. The divisions which have barred the way to this fellowship since the 16th century are removed. The participating churches are convinced that they have been put together in the one church of Jesus Christ, and that the Lord liberates them for, and lays upon them the obligation of, common service.

These statements clearly articulate the characteristics of "church fellowship" as one form of ecclesiastical union. They clearly show not

85. The English text of the Leuenberg Agreement can be found in William G. Rusch and Daniel F. Martensen, eds., *The Leuenberg Agreement and Lutheran-Reformed Relationships* (Minneapolis: Augsburg, 1989), 139–54.

only the specificity and the special concern of this model but also the more comprehensive form of this type of ecclesiastical union.

1. The brief definition of church fellowship establishes that it is a question of *communion between "churches of different confessional stances,"* with everything that this includes in differences of teaching, worship life, ecclesiastical order, piety, ethos. This difference of confessional stance is not transposed into transconfessionality and thus left behind. The "bond of the churches to their confessions" remains.[86] What is fundamentally changed is the relation between the different confessions, that is, the understanding of this relation. It is no longer separation but rather communion.

This is made possible by the development and binding reception of a "consensus." It does not replace existing confessions, but it shows that the diversity of confessions rests on an agreement about the core or fundamentals, on a common understanding of the gospel and of its correct transmission in the proclamation of the Word and in the sacraments. The churches "agree in the understanding of the gospel." According to Reformation conviction, only a disagreement in the understanding of the gospel can divide the churches; therefore, the consensus in the understanding of the gospel is necessary and also sufficient for the unity of the churches.[87] In view of this consensus, we find that the diversity of confessions is a difference between legitimate forms or formulations of the common understanding of the gospel that no longer separates.

On this basis, the churches' repudiation of one another's teachings can also be set aside. "The doctrinal condemnations no longer apply to the contemporary doctrinal position of the assenting churches."

2. The quoted text of the Agreement also shows that such a church fellowship of confessionally different churches corresponds to the understanding of unity that has taken shape in the ecumenical movement. The constitutive elements of visible unity are given: communion in faith, in the sacraments, in ministry, and in witness and service in the world.

86. "The Agreement leaves intact the binding force of the confessions within the participating churches" (no. 37).

87. Behind this clearly stands the Reformation understanding of the unity of the church as it is expressed especially in the *Confessio Augustana,* Article 7, as well as in the Second Helvetic Confession, Article 17.

It is precisely the last of these that must be emphasized. *"Communion in witness and service in the world"* belongs to the definition of church fellowship. Here is, in fact, an important refinement in and addition to the model of mutual recognition (see above 3.2.2.). The following text of the Leuenberg Agreement addresses this once more. Under "Witness and Service"[88] it states:

> The preaching of the churches gains credibility in the world when they are at one in their witness to the gospel. The gospel liberates and binds together the churches to render common service. Being the service of love, it turns to man in his distress and seeks to remove the causes of that distress. The struggle for justice and peace in the world increasingly demands of the churches the acceptance of a common responsibility.

Is the model of mutual recognition refined and completed also in terms of the *structural aspect* of ecclesiastical unity? (See 2.3.2.2.) A certain deficit becomes apparent here, so that at this point the Leuenberg understanding of ecclesiastical fellowship itself still needs refinement. The structural aspect is certainly not simply eliminated. It is said that "because of the intimate connection between witness and service, the church's service may call for formal legal unification."[89] Yet this is being left completely to the individual churches and the situations in which they live.[90]

A particular concern gave rise to this provision. Legal unification may lead to a "homogenization of preaching styles, worship life, church order, and diaconal as well as social activity that is detrimental to the essence of church fellowship."[91] The connection between commonality in the activities of the communion's witness and service, on the one hand, and in its structures, on the other, a commonality not only necessary for the visible unity of the church but also enabling those activities, is not sufficiently considered. This is not merely a matter of "consequences"[92] that might arise from the de-

88. Leuenberg Agreement, no. 36.

89. Leuenberg Agreement, no. 45.

90. Leuenberg Agreement, no. 44. "The question of organic union between particular churches can only be decided in the situation in which these churches live."

91. Leuenberg Agreement, no. 44.

92. Leuenberg Agreement, no. 42, "Organizational consequences."

clared church fellowship. Rather the structural element that corresponds to the ecumenical understanding of unity should be part of the nature of church fellowship and, therefore, of its definition. (Cf. above 2.3.2.2.)

The Leuenberg Agreement distinguishes between establishment or "declaration of church fellowship" and "realization of church fellowship." In this distinction, it wishes to show that church fellowship is not something static and given, but that it must "in the life of the churches and congregations become a reality" and needs to be "deepened and strengthened."[93] The understanding of church fellowship has a *historically dynamic dimension* that parallels the understanding of "united" churches as "uniting" churches. (Cf. 3.3.1.1.)

The effort for the "greatest possible commonality in witness and service in the world" belongs here but no less than the effort "to deepen further the common understanding of the gospel."[94] The Agreement calls the latter "the continuing theological task," and the churches signing the Agreement "pledge themselves to common doctrinal discussions."[95] In regard to these doctrinal conversations, it is a question, on the one hand, of further clarifications between existing, albeit not divisive, doctrinal differences and, on the other, of "problems . . . , recently emerging in regard to witness and service, order and practice."[96]

These doctrinal conversations take place and lead to regular "assemblies" of the signatory churches.[97] One can say that in these continuing doctrinal conversations something like structures of communion become visible.

93. Cf. Leuenberg Agreement, no. 35.

94. Leuenberg Agreement, no. 38.

95. Leuenberg Agreement, no. 37.

96. Leuenberg Agreement, nos. 39 and 40.

97. The results of the doctrinal conversations that have taken place so far (e.g., about the Two Kingdoms, Ministry and Ordination, Church, Doctrine and Practice of Holy Communion and Baptism) and the reports of the four assemblies have been published.

3.3.1.3. Parallel Roman Catholic Conceptions of the Model of Church Fellowship

Thus far, no model of union has been developed as such by the Roman Catholic Church; it is still a matter of ideas or concepts. Nonetheless, certain clear lines are discernible in the various Catholic comments. They point unmistakably to a model of union that is closely related to that of church fellowship, even though the Catholic elaboration of this model includes other elements in addition to those of a church fellowship between Reformation churches. Such elements correspond to the Catholic understanding of unity (cf. 2.2.5.) and include in particular communion in the office of bishop and communion with and under the bishop of Rome.

The key idea that determines this position was formulated by Joseph Ratzinger during the Second Vatican Council and prior to the promulgation of the Decree on Ecumenism:

> The idea of conversion that clearly has a place in relation to an individual whose conscience so directs her or him will be replaced basically by the idea of the unity of the churches that *remain churches* and yet *become one church*.[98]

Similarly, the General Synod of Catholic Dioceses in the Federal Republic of Germany (Würzburg, 1974) declared:

> It is quite acceptable to recognize in the multiplicity of traditions found in the different confessions also a legitimate multiplicity and to value it positively. The Synod hopes for a development in which the hitherto divisive contrasts are dismantled and overcome, and the churches and ecclesiastical communions hitherto separated become the bearers of the diverseness of the one church of Jesus Christ.[99]

The idea that there can be unity of the churches in which the uniqueness and relative independence of the individual churches is maintained is certainly nothing new for Catholic theology. It had already found application in the Union of Ferrara-Florence (1438–1439) between Latin and Byzantine churches, that is, with the for-

98. "Die Kirche und die Kirchen," in *Reformatio* 13, no. 2 (1964): 105.

99. *Synodenbeschlüsse: Pastorale Zusammenarbeit der Kirchen im Dienst an der christlichen Einheit,* 4.33; cf. 3.23 and 4.32.

mation of the churches of the East united with Rome.[100] It also governed the Malines Conversations (1921–1927) between the Anglican Church (Church of England) and the Roman Catholic Church.[101]

In both cases, it was not a question of a merger of the churches or an absorption of the non-Catholic churches into the Roman Catholic Church, even though in the case of the Uniate churches of the East, the tendency toward Latinization constantly intrudes in subsequent times. Irrespective of the communion in faith that was won (Decree of the Union of Florence) and the acknowledgment of papal primacy, each of the churches preserves its liturgical, canonical, and theological tradition, even its own episcopal jurisdiction. Even the common faith itself could be expressed in different formulations, for example, in view of the procession of the Spirit from the Father or from the Father and the Son *(filioque)*.

The newer Catholic considerations of models of unity are to be found in line with this.

a. The Concept of "Sister Churches"

Since the end of the 1960s, the concept of "sister churches" is mentioned repeatedly in the meetings and conversations of the Catholic Church especially with Orthodox and Anglican churches. As an expression for the relations between individual churches, it has a tradition reaching back to the early church.[102] Vatican II used it in this sense.[103] Since then, however, it has also been used as an expression for the regained communion between hitherto separated churches. The "message" of Paul VI to the Ecumenical Patriarch Athenagoras I on July 25, 1967, was important for this new linguistic usage. In that

100. See "Decree concerning Eastern Churches" in *(Orientalium Ecclesiarum) of the Second Vatican Council.* And recently: G. Alberigo, ed., *Christian Unity. The Council of Ferra-Florence 1438/39–1989* (Louvain: 1991).

101. Jacque de Bivort de la Saudée, *Documents sur le problème de l'union Anglo-Romaine (1921–1927)* (Paris: Pron, 1949), in particular the contributions of Dom Lambert Beauduin, *"L'église Anglicane unie, non absorbée,"* 212ff., and Bishop Gore, *"Unité avec la diversité,"* 275ff.

102. E. Lanne, OSB, |'Schwesterkirchen — Ekklesiologische Aspekte des Tomos Agapis," in *Auf dem Wege zur Einheit des Glaubens,* PRO ORIENTE (1976), 54ff.

103. *UR,* 14.

text, this concept was very consciously introduced in order to describe the relation between the Roman Catholic Church and the Orthodox Church.

> Today, after a long time of division and mutual misunderstanding, the Lord grants us that we again discover ourselves as sister churches in spite of the hindrances that were once erected between us.
>
> We need to come to know each other through genuine theological dialogue made possible by the renewal of fraternal love and to respect each other despite the legitimate differences in our liturgical, spiritual, and theological traditions and, finally, together sincerely confess all revealed truth.[104]

Some years later, Paul VI advocated the idea of "sister churches" also in view of a possible communion with the Anglican Church:

> There will be no attempt to lessen the legitimate prestige and the worthy patrimony of piety and usage, proper to the Anglican Church, when the Roman Catholic Church . . . is able to embrace her ever beloved sister in the one authentic communion of the family of Christ.[105]

b. The Concept of "Typos"

In a speech before representatives of the Anglican Church, Cardinal Willebrands, at that time President of the Secretariat for Unity, developed the thought that there are different ecclesiastical "types" (typoi), which are represented by individual churches or families of churches. They are connected with one another through fundamental commonalities but differ in specific forms of piety, teaching, ethos, canonical discipline, and ecclesiastical structures. Cardinal Willebrands defined the concept "typos" as follows:

> Where there is a long, coherent tradition, commanding men's love and loyalty, creating and sustaining a harmonious and organic whole of complementary elements, each of which supports and strengthens the other, you have the reality of a typos.

104. *AAS/59* (1967), 853f.
105. *Documents on Anglican-Roman Catholic Relations* (Washington: 1972), 42f.

The elements that constitute a special "typos" are "a characteristic theological method and view," a "characteristic liturgical expression," a specific "tradition of spirituality and devotion," and a "characteristic canonical discipline."

> The life of the church needs a variety of typoi, which would manifest the full catholic and apostolic character of the one and holy Church.[106]

c. *"Corporate Reunification"*

When the concept of "corporate unification" or "corporate reunification" is used in Catholic depictions of ecclesiastical unity, it is quite consistent with the idea of "sister churches" or that of "typos." It is the same term that, together with that of "organic union," played a significant role at the Conference of Edinburgh and thereafter. But it no longer refers to a transconfessional union of churches in which existing churches cease to be particular corporate bodies. This concept now refers to "reunification *as ecclesiastical corporate bodies*"[107] and to "a corporate unification in diversity" that preserves confessional uniqueness.[108]

This understanding of "corporate unification" or "corporate reunification" is often encountered in Catholic authors, especially in the 1970s.

> It (i.e., this kind of realization of unity) does not want to remove or level the evolved peculiarity of confessions still divided, but — irre-

106. "Speech in Cambridge, England, January 1970," in *Anglican-Roman Catholic Relations,* 38–41.

107. Bishop H. Tenhumberg, "Kirchliche Union bzw. korporative Wiedervereinigung," in *Kirche und Gemeinde: Hans Thimme zum 65. Geburtstag,* ed. W. Danielsmeyer and C. H. Ratschow (Witten: Luther-Verlag, 1974), 25. The predicate "corporate" refers not — as does the language of Edinburgh — to the "one body" that could be formed but to the different "corporate bodies" remaining in unity.

108. Thus J. Ratzinger in a lecture in 1976, republished in *Theologische Prinzipienlehre. Bausteine zur Fundamentaltheologie* (Munich: E. Wewel, 1982), 212. English translation in *Principles of Catholic Theology: Building Stones for a Fundamental Theology* (San Francisco: Ignatius, 1987), 201.

spective of the necessary unity — wants to confirm and integrate them in the full and unimpaired catholicity of the one church of Christ.[109]

3.3.1.4. The Debate Itself 1974–1978

The preliminary phase of the debate reveals the actual and necessary questions to be addressed. Two of the three basic models from the initial period of the ecumenical movement had developed further and also been applied concretely without clarification of their relationship. There was, in the first place, the model of organic union with its claim to be the only completely valid model of unity. There was also the model of mutual recognition — now in the form of the model of church fellowship and its parallel concepts — that, though it does not raise that claim for itself, disputes the exclusive claim of organic union.

The work of the Commission for Faith and Order and its "Vision of a United Church as Conciliar Fellowship" gave rise to the debate.

a. "The One Church as Conciliar Fellowship"

At its session in Louvain (1971), the first after the Assembly of the World Council of Churches in 1968 in Uppsala, the Commission on Faith and Order had concluded that one of the main focal points in its coming studies should be the theme of "concepts of unity and models of church union."[110] Different concerns came together here:[111] the clarification and evaluation of the existing and newly emerging understandings of unity and models of union; the determination of the relation between church union negotiations and bilateral dialogues; the further development of the New Delhi declaration of unity in light of the impulses of the Uppsala Assembly and especially its stress on the universal dimension of ecclesiastical unity. (See above 2.3.2.1.)

109. Bishop H. Tenhumberg, "Einheit der Christen. Fragen und Vorstellungen zur Wiedervereinigung," in *KNA — Ökumenische Information,* no. 10 (1978): 5.

110. Louvain (1971), Geneva, 239–40.

111. Geneva, 236–38.

The working session of the Commission in Salamanca (1973) was occupied with this. The core of its report on "The Next Steps on the Way to the Unity of the Church" is a description of the sought-after unity of the church as "conciliar fellowship," which was taken up at the following Assembly of the World Council of Churches at Nairobi (1975). It reads:

> The one Church is to be envisioned as a conciliar fellowship of local churches[112] which are themselves truly united. In this conciliar fellowship, each local church possesses, in communion with the others, the fullness of catholicity, witnesses to the same apostolic faith, and therefore recognizes the others as belonging to the same Church of Christ and guided by the same Spirit. As the New Delhi Assembly pointed out, they are bound together because they have received the same baptism and share in the same Eucharist; they recognize each other's members and ministries. They are one in their common commitment to confess the gospel of Christ by proclamation and service to the world. To this end, each church aims at maintaining sustained and sustaining relationships with her sister churches, expressed in conciliar gatherings whenever required for the fulfillment of their common calling.[113]

Does this explanation describe a model of ecclesiastical union in the sense of the models of union represented up to this point?

Although it is generally so perceived, it is only conditionally true. For the idea of "conciliar fellowship" expressed here does not claim to say in what form the hitherto divided churches — Lutheran, Reformed, Orthodox, Catholic, Anglican, and others — could be united with one another. It is much more a matter of how *already united churches* of a country or region can truly realize the unity of the church among themselves and hence on universal level rather than remaining isolated or even separated from one another. According to the declaration, this is where the idea of "conciliar fellowship" or communion has its place and function. It comes into effect only where and when on the local level, as defined above, the

112. The use of "local churches" here is somewhat unfortunate, for what is meant is not local parishes but larger units such as churches of a country or whole region.

113. Nairobi, 60.

unity of the church has already been achieved and the existing confessional divisions between churches and Christians have already been overcome. Thus, the declaration does not say anything initially about the unification of hitherto divided churches and offers no model of union as such, nor does it affect the controversy about models of union. This must be clearly understood.

Nevertheless, the idea of "conciliar fellowship" implies very clearly a model of union and thus could rekindle the debate about the models of union. It is the defining statement that conciliar fellowship is to be understood as a "communion of *local churches which are themselves truly united*" that is at issue here.

What this means is clearly stated in the Salamanca Report[114] and also later by the Commission on Faith and Order. "Local churches truly united" means churches united in the form of "organic union," to all of which applies what was said earlier about organic union, including particularly what was said in respect to its "transconfessionality."

The idea of "conciliar fellowship" or communion is thus most closely connected with the model of "organic union." The Salamanca Report expressly states this:

> The conciliar fellowship requires organic union. The vision of such a conciliar fellowship will, therefore, become a reality only as the churches are prepared to face, at all levels, the implications and challenge of organic union.[115]

So that no "misunderstanding" would arise on the matter, the Commission on Faith and Order repeated at its following session in Accra (1974): *"Conciliar fellowship requires organic union."*[116]

From this perspective, the view of "conciliar fellowship" intervenes in fact directly in the controversy about models of union. It repeats and renews the claim of the organic union model that it is the proper model of ecclesiastical union. And what "organic union" means is once again expressly stated at the Assembly of the World Council of Churches in Nairobi: "Organic union of separate denomi-

114. Salamanca Report, in Gassmann, *Documentary History of Faith and Order 1963-1993,* 41ff.

115. Gassmann, *Documentary History,* 41ff.

116. Faith and Order, Accra (1974), Geneva (1975), 67.

nations to form one body does mean a kind of death which threatens the denominational identity of its members."[117] It is "a kind of death" of confessional particularity and traditions through the melding of confessional churches into "one single corporate body."

b. "Unity in Reconciled Diversity"

The Salamanca Report contains a chapter about "the role of confessional world alliances in the ecumenical movement," about their bilateral dialogues and ecumenical engagement. Questions are put to the alliances, and they are asked to indicate how they see ". . . the relationship between, and respective functions of, the World Council of Churches and the Confessional World Alliances . . . how they can conceive their own role in relation to one another in the pursuit of unity in relation to the ecumenical movement. . . ." The desire was expressed for a "common basis for discussion" in the form of a "preparatory document" for the coming Assemblies of the World Council of Churches and of the individual alliances.

The confessional alliances accepted this request and in the course of 1974 held two consultations. The result was a "discussion paper" about "the ecumenical role of the confessional world alliances in the one ecumenical movement." In it the concept of "unity in reconciled diversity" is developed.[118]

> We consider the variety of denominational heritages legitimate insofar as the truth of the one faith explicates itself in history in a variety of expressions. We do not overlook the fact that such explications of the faith have been marked by error which has threatened the unity of the church. On the other hand, it needs to be seen that a heritage remains legitimate and can be preserved if it is properly translated into new historical situations. If it is, it remains a valuable contribution to the richness of life in the church universal. In the open encounter with other heritages the contribution of a particular denomination can lose its character of denominational exclusiveness. Therefore, unity and fellowship among the churches do not re-

117. Nairobi, 63.

118. The two chapters of the discussion papers in which it occurs are presented in G. Gassmann and H. Meyer, "Unity of the Church," 27–32 (see footnote 1 in ch. 3).

> quire uniformity of faith and order, but can and must encompass a plurality or diversity of convictions and traditions. This idea is as old as the ecumenical movement itself, but only in the last decade has it been taken seriously. (cf. Report of the Fourth Assembly of the World Council of Churches, Uppsala, 1968, Section I). On the basis of the old idea has emerged a new conception of the relationship between "confession" and "ecumenism." Confessional loyalty and ecumenical commitment are no contradiction, but are one — paradoxical as it may seem. When existing differences between churches lose their divisive character, there emerges a vision of unity that has the character of a "reconciled diversity."[119]

This view of "unity in reconciled diversity," like the idea of "conciliar fellowship," is not a real model of union. Yet this view of unity clearly corresponds to the basic model of "mutual recognition" or the model of "church fellowship" and relates itself to it. This is evident in the reference the discussion paper makes to the "Leuenberg Agreement" and the resultant church fellowship as an example of unity in reconciled diversity.[120]

Does the idea of reconciled diversity function as an alternative concept compared to and opposing that of conciliar fellowship? This is not the case, even if the subsequent discussion often perceived it in this way. The idea of a conciliar fellowship of churches is affirmed throughout. What is at issue is that the perception of a church as conciliar fellowship, as it is represented in the report of Salamanca, requires correction and expansion at a very specific point: where the idea of conciliar fellowship is joined one-sidedly and exclusively to the organic union model of uniting the churches. It is this junction of conciliar fellowship and organic union that is questioned. This is the concern, no more but also no less.

In other words, the idea of reconciled diversity makes a forceful plea that the "truly united local churches," which live with one another in the one church in conciliar fellowship, could also follow a model of union other than only the model of transconfessional organic union. It thus argues that another model of ecclesiastical union be placed alongside the model of organic union as one of

119. Gassmann and Meyer, "Unity of the Church," 31.
120. Gassmann and Meyer, "Unity of the Church," 31.

equal worth and of equal rights, one that preserves and protects the different confessional-ecclesiastical traditions and identities within the unity.

The Result of the Debate

The subsequent discussion was sharp, an indication that an important nerve of the whole question of the concept of the ecumenical aim had been touched. As it turned out, the discussion was carried on for the most part in terms of the materially skewed question of "conciliar fellowship or reconciled diversity," even though, on the whole, the real problem was clear all along. Is the ecumenical movement guided by an understanding of its aim that integrates and preserves the churches' unique characteristics and diversities arising from their history, or does it leave them aside?

It was to be expected that the subsequent Assembly of the World Council of Churches (Nairobi, 1975) would express favor for the idea of conciliar fellowship as understood in the Salamanca Report.[121] Still, it spoke also of another "tendency within the common commitment to unity . . . which lies in the primary stress . . . upon the necessity for faithfulness to the truth as it has been confessed in the past and as it is embodied in the received traditions." It is important that Nairobi regards these two "tendencies" as "not mutually exclusive."[122]

In contrast, the Assembly of the Lutheran World Federation in Dar es Salaam (1977) expressed itself in favor of the concept of reconciled diversity, as had also been expected. It developed it but stressed at the same time that it is "not to be set as an alternative over against the idea of 'conciliar fellowship' as it was developed in the framework of the World Council of Churches."[123]

The impulses for a mutual understanding that are apparent here came to fruition on three occasions in the year 1978: at the first "Forum on Bilateral Dialogue," at the meeting of the Commission on

121. Nairobi, 60.

122. Nairobi, 65.

123. Cf. Lutheran World Federation, *In Christ, A New Community,* 173–75 and 200.

Faith and Order in Bangalore, and at the consultation carried out for this purpose between representatives of the World Council of Churches and the confessional world alliances.[124]

The *result* can be summarized in three points:

First, there is the common affirmation of "the vision of the one church as a conciliar fellowship of local churches, which are themselves truly united." This is seen as an extension of the *common understanding of the unity of the church.* This common understanding of unity is the reference point for all models of ecclesiastical union, and in it lie also the "criteria for their assessment."[125] "Understanding of unity" and "models of union" are more clearly differentiated than previously. The one, common understanding of church unity does not necessarily require a single common model of ecclesiastical union. There can be different models of union, but the understanding of unity watches over and judges their legitimacy.

Second, this makes possible a differentiated answer to the central question, What are "truly united local churches" that come together in "conciliar fellowship"? It acknowledges that there are *two different models* — the texts speak of "concepts" or "ways of access" — which are designated by the two concepts of "organic union" and "unity in reconciled diversity," and which are characterized by *specific concerns* and accentuations. It states:

> Those placing emphasis on "organic union" want to stress that unity must be close enough to make possible the common witness at the local level. Those defending the concept "unity in reconciled diversity" want to promote the view that the confessional traditions, though they obviously need to be transformed, can have a continuing identifiable life within the one church.[126]

Third, each of these two models *corresponds to the common understanding of unity* of the church, just as it is expressed in the idea of the "one church as conciliar fellowship." Therefore, both models do not exclude each other.

124. Important texts that were developed on these three occasions appear in Gassmann and Meyer, "Unity of the Church," 33–54.

125. Cf. Gassmann and Meyer, "Unity of the Church," 33–34.

126. Gassmann and Meyer, "Unity of the Church," 52.

They may be two different ways of reacting to the ecumenical necessities and possibilities of different situations and of different church traditions.[127]

The Importance of the Achieved Agreement

Looking back over the decades-long discussion about the models of union with its strong and unresolved tensions, the importance of the achieved agreement is not to be underestimated. The discussion was, and is, not a question about pointless play with models. As has been pointed out at the beginning of this study, it was a question of whether the ecumenical movement, in itself very multiform, can be held together also and in particular by the vision of its aim and not break apart but rather preserve its inner unity and indivisibility (cf. above 1.1.).

On the basis of the New Delhi declaration of unity (1961), one can say that the ecumenical movement has come to a common understanding of the unity of the church, which informs it. Similarly, the debate of the 1970s has led to a clarification of the models of ecclesiastical union, at least in relation to two of the three basic models. Both are now accepted as legitimate models of union corresponding equally to the common understanding of unity, whose choice and use depend on the situations in which the churches live and on their own self-understanding.

Such an agreement was more urgent in the 1970s than ever before. Churches that, like the Orthodox churches and Roman Catholic Church, are formed by a strong consciousness of their uniqueness and tradition had entered into the ecumenical movement. At the same time, a unique and significant ecumenical role had fallen upon the confessional world alliances and especially their bilateral dialogues. These churches and ecclesiastical federations could integrate themselves fully and without reservation into the ecumenical movement only if its understanding of its aim did not contradict their self-understanding. This is precisely what the clarification of the relation between the transconfes-

127. Gassmann and Meyer, "Unity of the Church," 46.

sional and the confessional-bound basic model of church unification guaranteed.[128]

3.3.2. Bilateral Dialogues and Models of Union

Bilateral dialogues are, in principle, neutral in terms of models of union, although this requires certain restricting qualifications, as will be shown later. In this respect, such dialogues differ from negotiations or conversations about union. Formally speaking, the latter may, of course, be "bilateral conversations," but they are oriented from the outset by a particular model of ecclesiastical unification, namely, that of organic union (cf. 3.3.1.1.).

Bilateral dialogues generally do not commence with reflections about the appropriate form of realizing ecclesiastical unity between the partners. They, first of all, concentrate totally on a better mutual understanding and discussion of outstanding controversial questions between the dialogue partners. It is part of the inner dynamic of the dialogues, however, that the more the church-dividing differences recede, the closer they approach the question of the models of union and finally are confronted with this issue.

This points out the strong tendency of bilateral dialogues to a confession-related model of union, that is, to the basic model of mutual recognition (cf. 3.2.2.). The decision to engage in "bilateral" conversations appears in this respect to contain in itself something like a predecision. In any case, there are few bilateral dialogues which have turned into union conversations or union negotiations in the specific sense.[129]

There clearly is restraint in the use of terminology. Rarely is there a firm commitment to any one of the technical terms like "church fellowship" or "unity in reconciled diversity." Rather the envisioned

128. The consultation of the World Council of Churches and the confessional world alliances of 1978 declared, therefore, that the "difference expressed in these two concepts does not prevent the churches from undertaking together concrete steps on the road of unity" (in Gassmann and Meyer, "Unity of the Church," 52).

129. The present discussions and negotiations between the Reformed and Lutheran churches in Holland, which aim at the formation of a united Protestant church in that country, appear to be an exception. As is stated there on occasion, the intent is "to go beyond Leuenberg."

form of church unification is circumscribed and depicted in terms of other concepts. Nonetheless, the terms "recognition" and "to acknowledge" recur again and again as central terms, pointing clearly to the basic model of "mutual recognition."

There are numerous examples of this among the bilateral dialogues, especially on the national and regional but also international levels.

National/Regional Dialogues

The conversations in *Europe* between *Lutherans and Reformed churches,* which explicitly accepted in their final phase the model of "church fellowship" and actualized it with the Leuenberg Agreement, are an especially clear example of this, as has been already described (see above 3.3.1.2.).

In the *United States,* the situation was quite similar in the conversations between *Episcopalians* (Anglicans) *and Lutherans* and between *Lutherans and Reformed,* conversations which, after a long period, appear now to have entered their final phase.

The first of these two conversations in the United States has proposed a "Concordat of Agreement" that establishes "full communion" between the Episcopal Church and the Evangelical Lutheran Church in America (ELCA).[130] The concept of "full communion" is expressly understood in the sense of the report of the Joint Anglican/Lutheran Working Group (1983) (see 2.3.2.4.).[131] It states:

> By full communion we here understand a relationship between two distinct churches or communions. Each maintains its own autonomy and recognizes the catholicity and apostolicity of the other, and each believes the other to hold the essentials of the Christian faith.[132]

130. W. A. Norgren and W. G. Rusch, eds., *"Towards Full Communion" and "Concordat of Agreement." Lutheran-Episcopal Dialogue, series III* (Minneapolis: Augsburg, 1991).

131. Norgren and Rusch, eds., *"Towards Full Communion,"* 72f.

132. See "Report of the Anglican-Lutheran Joint Working Group, Cold Ash, Berkshire, England — 1983," in *What Can We Share: A Lutheran-Episcopal Resource and Study Guide,* comp. by William A. Norgren (Cincinnati: Forward Movement Publications, 1985), 90.

The conversation between Lutherans and Reformed has developed a "model of mutual affirmation and admonition" that should be realized through a "Formula of Agreement" similar to the Leuenberg Agreement.[133] The text states:

> Replacing the polemics and formal condemnations of earlier times, our model of mutual affirmation and admonition within a fellowship of churches recognizing their unity in the understanding of the gospel and of the gift of the sacraments provides a framework for continuing theological reflection without the need of perpetuating the existing divisions.[134]

The decades-long conversations between the *Evangelical Church of Germany (EKD) and the Church of England* also led in 1988 to a communion of "mutual recognition" of both churches, which, since full communion in ecclesiastical office (ministry) has yet to be achieved, is not always seen as the realization of "full visible unity."[135] The declaration states:

> We recognize one another's churches as churches belonging to the One, Holy, Catholic and Apostolic Church of Jesus Christ and truly participating in the apostolic mission of the whole people of God;
>
> we acknowledge that in our churches the Word of God is authentically preached and the sacraments of baptism and Eucharist are duly administered;
>
> we acknowledge one another's ordained ministries as given by God and instruments of his grace, and look forward to the time when the reconciliation of our churches makes possible the full interchangeability of ministers. . . .[136]

In the relations and conversations between the *Church of England and the Lutheran Churches of Northern Europe* (Scandinavia and the Baltic countries), which can look back on a long history, the realiza-

133. K. F. Nickle and T. F. Lull, eds., *A Common Calling. The Witness of Our Reformation Churches in North America Today* (Minneapolis: 1993).

134. Nickle and Lull, *Common Calling,* 40, cf. 34, 66, and above.

135. Church of England. Board for Mission and Unity, *On the Way to Visible Unity, Meissen, 1988* (London: General Synod of the Church of England, 1988), esp. 22–28 (Chapter VI: "Mutual Acknowledgement and Next Steps").

136. Church of England, *On the Way,* 22.

tion of full visible unity with one another appears imminent. The "Common Statement of Porvoo" (1992) made this possible.[137] Here too the "Joint Declaration" at the end of the complete text is, in its decisive aspects, a mutual "acknowledgment" among the churches, followed by "commitments" relating to their life together. The actual "Declaration" uses language that, while in part is identical with that of the "Meissen Declaration," also goes beyond it.

> We acknowledge one another's churches as churches belonging to the One, Holy, Catholic and Apostolic Church of Jesus Christ and truly participating in the apostolic mission of the whole people of God;
>
> we acknowledge that in all our churches the Word of God is authentically preached, and the sacraments of baptism and the Eucharist are duly administered;
>
> we acknowledge that all our churches share in the common confession of the apostolic faith;
>
> we acknowledge that one another's ordained ministries are given by God as instruments of his grace and as possessing not only the inward call of the Spirit, but also Christ's commission through his body, the Church;
>
> we acknowledge that personal, collegial and communal oversight (episcope) is embodied and exercised in all our churches in a variety of forms, in continuity of apostolic life, mission and ministry;
>
> we acknowledge that the episcopal office is valued and maintained in all our churches as a visible sign expressing and serving the Church's unity and continuity in apostolic life, mission and ministry.[138]

Here also is the key concept of "mutual recognition."

International Dialogues

The dialogues between the worldwide church communions or churches are, all in all, much more reserved in regard to models of

137. "The Porvoo Common Statement," in *Together in Mission and Ministry* (London: Church House Publishing, 1993).

138. "Porvoo," 30f.

unification. Among these international dialogues, only one has thus far intentionally occupied itself with it, that is to say, the Catholic-Lutheran dialogue. Wherever they approach this question, however, the tendency toward the basic model of mutual recognition, which characterizes the national/regional bilateral conversation, is clearly noticeable.

In some of the dialogues, it is obvious that the "koinonia" concept is used in this sense. The importance of "koinonia" then moves, so to speak, from its primary ecclesiological meaning (church as koinonia) to the ecumenical meaning, which is related to the understanding of unity (unity of the church as koinonia; see 2.3.2.4.) and, finally, to the area of models of union.

This becomes especially clear in the *Methodist-Catholic dialogue*, where "possible forms of the unity of the church" are mentioned.[139] It states:

> We have found that koinonia both as a concept and an experience is more important than any particular model of church union that we are yet able to propose.

What is intended here is more clearly explained by reference to the ideas of "typos" and of "sister churches" (see 3.3.1.3.), to the unions of Ferrara-Florence (see 3.3.1.3.), and to John Wesley, who perceived his movement as an analogy to the "religious orders in the one church" with their "special forms of life and prayer, of work, of evangelism and . . . organization" and in "relative independence . . . within the unity of the church."

One may say that it is similar in the *Anglican-Catholic dialogue*, even if that dialogue itself is consciously reserved in the exact description of its goal.

In the context and at the end of a detailed reflection about the koinonia/communio understanding of the church, which is said to be fundamental for the entire dialogue,[140] the introduction of the concluding report speaks of "the full visible communion between our two churches" as the goal of the dialogue. What this means is

139. "Report of the Methodist-Roman Catholic Dialogue of 1985, a Statement on the Church," in *Information Service — The Secretariat for Promoting Christian Unity* 4, no. 62 (1986): 209.

140. Meyer and Vischer, eds., *Growth in Agreement*, 65–67.

not developed in detail; nonetheless, it is stated that this "full visible communion" cannot exist "without mutual recognition of the sacraments and ministry."[141] Here the key concept of "recognition" is used.

The affirmation of continuing diversity contained in the concept of recognition and consistently emphasized in every individual document from the Anglican-Catholic dialogue appears especially in the context of the issue of primacy. If Anglicans are ready to concede universal primacy to the bishop of Rome, then it is a primacy that serves the churches' koinonia, whose "jurisdiction preserves and joins together the riches of the diverse traditions," and which for Anglicans would "not involve the suppression of theological, liturgical, and other traditions which they value or the imposition of wholly alien traditions."[142]

It is apparent that the present-day Anglican-Catholic dialogue proceeds along the lines of the Malines Conversations (1921–1927) and their motto of an "Anglican church united with but not absorbed by" the Roman Catholic Church.[143] The reference to "the sister churches," which Paul VI made in relation to the goal of the Anglican-Catholic dialogue (see 3.3.1.3.),[144] belongs here as does the "typos" concept that Cardinal Willebrands developed in his address before representatives of the Anglican Church (see above 3.3.1.3.).

The Anglican *"Emmaus Report"* formulates this when it refers to the "aim" of the Anglican-Catholic dialogue in the following statement: "Such a unity would be one of relationship rather than identity."[145]

"Full communion" is also the concept with which the international *Anglican-Lutheran dialogue* describes its goal. Here too "full communion" is described as the "relation between two different

141. Meyer and Vischer, eds., *Growth in Agreement,* 67.

142. Meyer and Vischer, eds., *Growth in Agreement,* 112.

143. See 3.3.1.3., footnote 101. Paul VI quoted this phrase in his speech on the occasion of the visit of the Archbishop of Canterbury (May 15, 1977; *AAS* 69 [1977], 284).

144. The dialogue itself refers to this statement of Paul VI (No. 22). See Meyer and Vischer, eds., *Growth in Agreement,* 122.

145. Anglican Ecumenical Consultation (1987: West Wickham, England), *The Emmaus Report. A Report of the Anglican Ecumenical Consultation 1987* (London: Church House Publishing, 1987), 46.

churches or communions." The statements that are important for our context and which are more precisely developed in the text are these:

> By full communion we here understand a relationship between two distinct churches or communions. Each maintains its own autonomy and recognizes the catholicity and apostolicity of the other, and each believes the other to hold the essentials of the Christian faith. . . . To be in full communion means that churches become interdependent while remaining autonomous.[146]

It adds that such full communion between different and independent churches can, indeed, develop into a "uniting of ecclesial bodies," that is to say, into a church union:

> It may lead to a uniting of ecclesial bodies if they are, or come to be, immediately adjacent in the same geographical area. This should not imply the suppressing of ethnic, cultural or ecclesial characteristics or traditions which may in fact be maintained and developed by diverse institutions within one communion.[147]

As already mentioned, among the international bilateral dialogues, the Catholic-Lutheran conversation has dealt explicitly and most extensively with the question of the models of union.[148]

It offers, first of all, a brief description of models of union represented in the ecumenical discussion and then describes in light of this, but without adopting a specific model, the "shaping of Catholic-Lutheran church fellowship."[149] The decisive section, the more detailed elucidation of which is supported by everything that follows it, states:

> The unity we seek will be a unity in diversity. Particularities developed within the two traditions will not merely be fused, nor their differences completely given up. . . .

146. "Anglican-Lutheran Relations," 90–91.

147. "Anglican-Lutheran Relations," 91–92.

148. This is documented in Joint Lutheran/Roman Catholic Study Commission, *Facing Unity* of 1984, the official edition of which had the subtitle *Models, Forms and Phases of Catholic-Lutheran Church Fellowship.*

149. Joint Lutheran/Roman Catholic Study Commission, *Facing Unity,* 7–20.

> What is really at stake is that a theologically based agreement of the type that already exists in the Catholic-Lutheran dialogue should work through divergences to the point where they lose their church divisive character. At the same time it should both clarify and make certain that remaining differences are based on a fundamental consensus in understanding the apostolic faith and therefore are legitimate. . . .
>
> Once the divergences of both traditions have lost their divisive force, they can no longer be the subject of mutual condemnation. It should be publicly declared that they are now groundless. . . .
>
> The unity we seek must be rooted in common sacramental life. . . .
>
> The unity we seek must assume concrete form in suitable structures that would enable our hitherto separated communities to lead a truly common life and to make joint action possible both at the level of the local churches and at the universal level. . . .
>
> In our endeavours to find appropriate structures needed for full and binding fellowship we shall have to face up to the question of jointly exercising ministry of church leadership, present in the office of bishop in the Early Church.[150]

This form of ecclesiastical union also clearly comes under the scope of the basic model of mutual recognition.[151]

The situation is different only in the *Anglican-Reformed dialogue*. When it speaks of "our aim" and "form of unity," the view is expressly rejected that "the form of visible unity sought is the reconciliation of these denominations in such a way as to enable them to continue to exist in their present form while recognizing and accepting one another as optional alternative manifestations of the one holy catholic church."[152]

150. Joint Lutheran/Roman Catholic Study Commission, *Facing Unity*, 21–22.

151. To be sure, it is expressly said at the same time that the realization of communion cannot happen by mere "recognition" of the other in its particularity. A process of "reception" must appear, i.e., the "process to accept and appropriate that which is special for the other, as far as it represents a contribution to one's proper life and thought, and is considered necessary for the realization of communion." "Recognition" and "reception" are an integral process in the realization of church fellowship. Joint Lutheran/Roman Catholic Study Commission, *Facing Unity*, 23.

152. *God's Reign and Our Unity. The Report of the Anglican-Reformed International Commission 1984*, nos. 106 and 110 (London: 1984).

Instead of this, however, there is a decisive plea for the model of organic union, that is, of "united churches" in which the confessional or denominational differences are overcome and left behind.[153]

> Since we see the denomination not as by itself "the Church," but as a family or fellowship of churches, we are agreed that Christian unity must in the last resort be discovered and actualized at the local level. Hence we seek the emergence of reconciled local communities, each of which is recognized as "church" in the proper sense. . . .[154]

3.3.3. The Subsequent Theological Discussion

The debate about models of union really took place within the institutional framework of the ecumenical movement, that is, in the context of ecumenical conferences, interchurch dialogues and negotiations, ecumenical commissions and consultations. Nevertheless, at least at times it has prompted a further theological discussion, which can be portrayed here only very basically.

Specific models of union, as they were represented in the earlier material, did not stand in the center of this discussion. The central issue above all was the problem of unity and diversity. To be sure, it was no longer a question of the mere "understanding" of ecclesiastical unity but rather of its concrete realization. How can unity be realized and lived in the perduring diversity of the churches and confessions? This was, as it were, the key question. The discussion thus addressed the question of ecclesiastical "union," but without repeating the discussion of the nature of "unity." It presupposed rather what had been said fundamentally in that context about unity and diversity and had been gained in insights.

The noteworthy theological contributions here derive from the 1980s.

153. *God's Reign,* nos. 179–80.

154. *God's Reign,* no. 110.

The "Fries-Rahner Plan"

The first and probably most discussed of these contributions is the joint work of H. Fries and K. Rahner, *The Unity of the Churches: An Actual Possibility.*[155] The Fries-Rahner "model" of ecclesiastical union, which explicitly understands itself as a form of "reconciled diversity,"[156] can be summarized in the following way.

For all churches and confessions, the "fundamental truths of Christianity" are obligatory, as they are expressed in the Holy Scripture, in the apostolic confession of faith, and in the confession of Nicaea and Constantinople. Herein exists that "unity of faith" between the churches necessary for church communion. Beyond these "fundamental truths," no dogma of an individual church is to be made obligatory for the other churches, and no church is allowed to reject outright the binding teaching of the other churches. Thus the diversities of teaching will remain but will at the same time be neutralized, insofar as universal epistemological reasons prevent us from making judgments about them. Communion between doctrinally, liturgically, and structurally independent churches is guaranteed institutionally by the office of bishop, which exists in or is to be accepted by all churches, as well as by the common acknowledgment of the Petrine ministry of the Bishop of Rome. He, on his part, so exercises this ministry that the uniqueness and independence of the churches are recognized and respected. Within this communion that extends to every dimension of life in the church, every church will understand ordination such that mutual recognition of ministries and communion of pulpit and table among the churches are possible.[157]

155. Quaestiones Disputatae 100 (Freiburg/Basel/Vienna: Herder, 1983). A "special edition" of the year 1985 includes as an appendix a detailed analysis of the subsequent discussion. The English edition is H. Fries and K. Rahner, *Unity of the Churches: An Actual Possibility* (Philadelphia: Fortress Press, 1985).

156. H. Fries and K. Rahner, *Unity of the Churches,* 36–37, 62, 66, 108–9.

157. Fries and Rahner themselves summarize their plan of union in eight theses which they put at the beginning of their work (*Unity of the Churches,* 7–10). They then take these theses up one after the other and develop them.

The "Evangelical Counterproposal" of E. Herms

In his work, *Einheit der Christen in der Gemeinschaft der Kirchen,* E. Herms submits the Fries-Rahner plan to a detailed critique.[158] At the same time, he develops his own plan or model of the communion of churches as an "evangelical counterproposal."[159]

Herms holds a more radical view of the difference between Catholic and Reformation churches. In relation to revelation and its transmission, there exists between them a "fundamental difference of conviction" that has the character of a "contradictory opposition"[160] or "contradictory opposition of doctrine."[161] This difference is determinative for both churches but particularly for the Protestant churches. For that reason, its harshness cannot be overcome, reconciled, or even just toned down and, hence, cannot tolerate the "epistemological tolerance" that Fries and Rahner advocate. Rather, this difference calls for opposition.

Nevertheless, according to Herms, ecclesiastical communion is possible, namely, through "mutual renunciation of excommunication" and "mutual recognition," which then would be ratified by the "resumption of table fellowship."[162] For Herms such a unity with "contradictory opposition" — he calls it "ecumenical-constructive tension"[163] — is quite conceivable in that he understands the "fundamental difference of conviction" between Catholic and Protestant thought as "two ways of the Spirit's action," which are "to be respected as providential."[164]

158. Eilert Herms, *Die ökumenische Bewegung der römischen Kirche im Lichte der reformatorischen Theologie. Antwort auf den Rahner-Plan* (Göttingen: Vandenhoeck and Ruprecht, 1984).

159. Herms, *Die ökumenische Bewegung der römischen Kirche,* 181–201.

160. Herms, *Die ökumenische Bewegung der römischen Kirche,* 184, 186, and above.

161. Herms, *Die ökumenische Bewegung der römischen Kirche,* 200.

162. Herms, *Die ökumenische Bewegung der römischen Kirche,* 199f.

163. Herms, *Die ökumenische Bewegung der römischen Kirche,* 189.

164. Herms, *Die ökumenische Bewegung der römischen Kirche,* 192.

"Communion in Opposites"

The idea of a communion of churches fraught with high internal tension appears elsewhere as well. The term one now encounters again and again is "communion in opposites," an unambiguous and quite deliberate intensification of the term "unity in diversity."

The work of E. Geldbach, *Ökumene in Gegensätzen,*[165] and the article by L. Klein, "Theologische Alternative zur Konsens Ökumene," come to mind in particular.[166] Reference should also be made to certain parts of the paper *Theologie der Ökumene — Ökumenische Theoriebildung* of the German Ecumenical Study Group, to which both of the authors mentioned belong.[167]

In contrast to Herms, the point of departure in this approach is, above all else, the churches' reception of the consensus of doctrine that the dialogues had tried to reach and that had been experienced as very difficult to reach and had, indeed, failed. This provides impetus for a new, critical reflection on the method and aim of the churches' efforts on behalf of unity. The question raised is whether the ecumenical efforts to date were not oriented toward "an aim far too lofty,"[168] namely, one ultimately determined by notions of conformity, of theological consensus and ecclesiastical unity.

In contrast, another concept of the aim is now being developed, one that is understood as an alternative to "visible ecclesiastical unity"[169] or "consensus ecumenism."[170] For both authors as well as for the paper of the German Ecumenical Study Group, this alternative is the "communion" or "unity in opposites."[171] The intent is finally not to do away with the existing diversities between the churches through efforts for theological consensus. The existing diversities, contrasts, and contradictions, indeed, even the mutual condemnations and rejections[172] are left as they are, the allegation being that despite the

165. Bensheimer Heft 66 (Göttingen: Vandenhoeck und Ruprecht, 1987).

166. In *ThQ* 1986/4, 268–78.

167. In *ÖR* 1988/2, 205–22.

168. Geldbach, "Baptists and the Ecumenical Movement," 120.

169. Geldbach, "Baptists and the Ecumenical Movement," 120, cf. 115.

170. L. Klein, "Theologische Alternative zur Konsens Ökumene." See the title of his article and 277f.

171. Klein, 277f.; German Ecumenical Study Group (see footnote 167 in ch. 3), esp. 207f., 213; Geldbach, "Baptists and the Ecumenical Movement," 115, 117, 126.

172. Klein, 277.

contrasts and contradictions there can be "communion in prayer and worship."[173] The existing opposites are even viewed as "creative" and "belonging to the life of Christianity."[174]

This "communion in opposites" is realized and takes place in a "continuous dialogue." Dialogue is now no longer simply the "means to unity"[175] or the "preliminary stage for koinonia."[176] Dialogue is "expression and structural elements of ecumenical communion,"[177] indeed, the "consummation of unity" itself.[178] The requisite "dynamic, cybernetic function" in this process is exercised for Geldbach, a man of Free Church tradition, by an institute for the "interlinking" and "synchronization of dialogues," a "secretariat for dialogue,"[179] while for the Catholic Klein this is done by the "offices" or ministries of the church.[180]

O. Cullmann: "Unity through Diversity"

A writing which in many respects is quite different but still belongs in this context is that of O. Cullmann.[181] It starts with a New Testa-

173. Klein, 277.

174. Klein, 277.

175. Klein, 276.

176. Geldbach, "Baptists and the Ecumenical Movement," 118.

177. Geldbach, "Baptists and the Ecumenical Movement," 118.

178. Klein, 277; German Ecumenical Study Group, 218. Passing reference must be made here to the passage in Ch. Link, U. Luz, and L. Fischer, *Sie aber hielten fest an der Gemeinschaft . . . Einheit der Kirche als Prozess im Neuen Testament und heute* (Zurich: Benziger, 1988). As the title already states, a concept of the ecumenical aim is developed here that consistently understands the unity of the church as a continuous and changing "process" (esp. 187–94). They speak literally of a process model (259), which takes the place of the understanding of unity and of the models of union held until now that all are informed by the aim of reaching visible unity. Only the model of "conciliar fellowship," of a council as "instrument of the process" (261), is kept.

179. Klein, 277.

180. Geldbach, "Baptists and the Ecumenical Movement," 118f.

181. Oscar Cullmann, *Unity through Diversity: Its Foundation, and a Contribution to the Discussion concerning the Possibilities of Its Actualization* (Philadelphia: Fortress Press, 1988). The original German edition appeared in 1986 with the title *Einheit durch Vielfalt.* A second German edition was published in 1990 with an additional chapter dealing with the reactions to the first edition.

ment foundation, then asks about the practical realization of unity in diversity and finally deals with new ecumenical designs.

The title of the work is programmatic: not unity "in spite of" diversity but "unity through diversity."[182] The book is primarily concerned with demonstrating through recourse to the New Testament what such unity is.[183] ". . . [W]here the Holy Spirit is at work in accord with its true nature, diversifying plurality is generated within this unity . . . whoever . . . wants uniformity . . . sins against the Holy Spirit."[184] When seen in this light, "every Christian confession has a permanent spiritual gift, a charisma, which it should preserve, nurture, purify, and deepen, and which should not be given up for the sake of homogenization."[185]

On the basis of this, Cullmann develops a proper model, a "plan" or "proposal" of unity,[186] as he puts it. "What I propose is a real community of completely independent churches that remain Catholic, Protestant, and Orthodox, that preserve their spiritual gifts, not for the purpose of excluding each other, but for the purpose of forming a *community of all churches that call on the name of our Lord Jesus Christ.*"[187] Such a communion of churches needs "visible actualization . . . especially with regard to structure."[188] Without flatly rejecting the idea of a unifying Petrine ministry proposed by Fries-Rahner, Cullmann still advocates a model of a council independent of the Pope.[189]

Occasionally, there are formulations in the first edition in which Cullmann's model appears to approach that of "communion in opposites," for example, when he speaks of a "fellowship of churches remaining divided." Yet in the second edition, which has not appeared in an English translation, Cullmann has expressly withdrawn the attribute "divided" *(getrennt)* and speaks instead throughout of "independent" *(eigenständigen)* or "autonomous" *(autonomen)* churches.[190]

182. Cullmann, *Unity through Diversity,* 16.
183. Cullmann, *Unity through Diversity,* 11.
184. Cullmann, *Unity through Diversity,* 16–17.
185. Cullmann, *Unity through Diversity,* 9.
186. Cullmann, *Unity through Diversity,* 49, 64, and 81.
187. Cullmann, *Unity through Diversity,* 33.
188. Cullmann, *Unity through Diversity,* 36.
189. Cullmann, *Unity through Diversity,* 64.
190. Cullmann, *Unity through Diversity,* 2nd ed., 10f.

Summary

From the perspective of the long ecumenical debate about the models of ecclesiastical union, as described in the preceding sections, this theological discussion appears to have been of little help in advancing matters, however stimulating it may have been.

It certainly has contributed to the complete abandonment of a monolithic understanding of ecclesiastical unity and to deepening the conviction of the legitimate diversity to be preserved in unity. This is especially true of the work of O. Cullmann. What is unsatisfying about this discussion, however, also emerges precisely at this point.

The idea of legitimate and necessary diversity seems in most of the contributions to have such a preponderance that the critical question about the limits of diversity and with it the struggle for overcoming church-dividing differences — an absolutely central and necessary concern of the ecumenical movement — recedes into the background.

This is the case when Fries and Rahner place doctrinally controversial questions between the churches under the principle of epistemological tolerance and call for abstention of judgment.[191] The "evangelical counterproposal" of Herms is not free from this same concern when he considers church-communion to be possible even with "contradictory doctrinal opposition" and "contradictory oppositions." All the more is it the case when some, such as Geldbach and Klein, give up doctrinal consensus and efforts for consensus altogether and are content with a "communion in opposites" or declare the principle of unity to be the process of dialogue that has been released from achieving consensus.

Such ideas and proposals can scarcely, if at all, be made to correspond to the understanding of unity that determines the ecumenical movement and to which the models of ecclesiastical union must correspond.

191. On the basis of critical questions, Fries later responded to this point: "The concept of existential-epistemological tolerance and the abstention of judgment resulting from it is not free from misunderstanding; it could and should be clarified by a more adequate redescription in the sense of a factual-positive judgment" (special, expanded edition [see footnote 155 above] of Quaestiones Disputatae, 169).

3.3.4. The "Conciliar Process" and the Question of Models of Ecclesiastical Union

Origin and Significance of the Conciliar Process

In the preceding sections it was shown that two of those three "basic models" of church union, which reached prominence already in the initial phases of the ecumenical movement, have held their own into the present, been further developed, and also applied. Can that also be said in relation to the third model, the "cooperative-federal model" (cf. 3.2.1.)?

The following two characteristics distinguish this model (see 3.2.1.).

First, it is characterized above all by its primary orientation to the common action of Christians and churches toward the world. This means common action that is not ad hoc and can be canceled any time the occasion calls for it but rather common action that is encompassing, obliging, and meant for the long haul. "Federal" interecclesial structures are to serve this end.

Second — and the concepts of "federation" and "federal" refer to this — this model preserves the independence and identity of the different churches. Common action directed to the world, so it is believed, does not necessarily require the surrender of ecclesiastical independence and confessional identity.

As it turned out, neither feature finally caused the cooperative-federal model and its advocates to declare the need for the churches' unity in faith, sacrament, and ministry and the effort to achieve it to be a secondary matter, not to speak of relegating it into irrelevance. In its primary orientation toward the common action of Christians and churches in the world, this model of union put emphasis on a deeply felt concern in the ecumenical movement from its very beginning. It did so, however, not necessarily at the expense of other aspects of ecclesiastical unity and stayed, therefore, within the contours of the understanding of visible unity that gives orientation to the ecumenical movement as a whole.

At the Assembly of the World Council of Churches in Uppsala (1968), the theme of the common mission of the church to the world was reinforced emphatically (see above 2.3.2.3.). In the subsequent debate of the 1970s about the models of union, however, it receded in a remarkable manner.

The Vancouver Assembly (1983) brought about a clear change in this respect. It gathered together different socioethical studies, activities, and programs in which the World Council and its member churches had been previously engaged and called for a "conciliar process of mutual commitment for justice, peace, and the integrity of creation." It was decided that in the future this must be one of the "focal points" of the work of the World Council of Churches and its member churches. Vancouver puts it as follows:

> To engage member churches in a conciliar process of mutual *commitment (covenant) to justice, peace and the inegrity of all creation* should be a priority for World Council programmes. The foundation of this emphasis should be confessing Christ as the life of the world and Christian resistance to the demonic powers of death in racism, sexism, caste oppression, economic exploitation, militarism, violations of human rights, and the misuse of science and technology.[192]

The positive answer in the churches and among Christians was strong, especially in the churches of the Third World but also in other countries, not least in Germany. This could hardly be otherwise. The grave dangers that today really threaten the existence of humankind — the accelerating social and economic injustice under which the overwhelming majority of human beings live, the danger of war aggravated by weapons of mass destruction, and the ecological threat to the world — were all taken into consideration so that they could be resisted by means of a firm and, indeed, formal, mutual commitment, based on common convictions of Christian faith.

The "process" quickly gained in breadth. It became a kind of movement within the ecumenical movement that also powerfully affected traditional forms of ecumenical effort, reminding them emphatically and critically that the aim of the ecumenical movement was not limited to the reconciliation between churches.

The breadth of the "process" was manifested by its bearers, the countless base groups that often were bound together in ecumenical

192. David Gill, ed., *Gathered for Life: Official Report, VI Assembly World Council of Churches, Vancouver, Canada, 24 July–10 August 1983* (Geneva: World Council of Churches, 1983), 255.

networks as well as the official churches themselves. This breadth was also apparent in the sometimes tense diversity of foci and priorities which were themselves usually shaped by context, but all taking place within the threefold direction of the overall process, namely, justice, peace, creation. Finally, the breadth was apparent in the plethora of concrete aims and projects.

The idea of "conciliarity" was important, even though it met with reservations in situations where one felt committed to the classical concept of council. "Conciliar assemblies" were akin to concentrations or conjunctions and were a necessary structural instrument of the continuing "process of mutual commitment." Through those assemblies, the process gained greater visibility and cohesion while, at the same time, keeping its form as a process.

Such conciliar assemblies or gatherings occurred again and again in different countries and regions. The European ecumenical assembly "Peace in Justice" in Basel (1989)[193] and the world assembly "Justice, Peace, Integrity of Creation" in Seoul (1990)[194] were especially well known and important with their final documents and the common "commitments" and "covenants" they contain.

The Conciliar Process — No "Model for Ecclesiastical Union"

In the context of this study, the importance of the conciliar process and its concerns is not at issue. There can be no questions about this. Nor is it a question of its internal problems or *aporiae,* of the external difficulties and resistance it encounters, of how it sustains itself, what it has managed to or even can accomplish, and what effects it has.

Here the question is how the conciliar process fits into the ecumenical movement with its declared aim of the visible unity of the churches, or more exactly, whether the conciliar process so fits into

193. European Ecumenical Assembly (1989: Basel, Switzerland), *Frieden in Gerechtigkeit. Dokumente der Europäischen Ökumenischen Versammlung* (Basel: F. Reinhardt, 1989), the official documents of the European Ecumenical Assembly 1989 in Basel. See the final document *Frieden in Gerechtigkeit für die ganze Schöpfung,* 43-48.

194. *Justice, Peace, Integrity of Creation,* Final Document of the World Assembly, Seoul, Korea, March 6–12, 1990. World Council of Churches. Central Committee, Document No. 19.

the ecumenical movement that it may be regarded as a form or "model" of the realization of this aim as it was understood and described in the ecumenical movement.

This question raises strong doubts, however much the conciliar process and its concerns may and should be confirmed and be participated in energetically. Given how the process has presented itself to date and developed up to the two great conciliar gatherings in Basel and Seoul, one must conclude that in it the *problem* of the church's visible unity and the *effort* to achieve it — in the sense of an effort for the communion of churches in faith, teaching, and order — is marginal, even overlooked.

Note well that what is marginal and overlooked is certainly not the unity of the churches and Christians in faith as such. The "conciliar process of mutual commitment" absolutely requires a certain communion in faith among Christians and churches and grows from it, as the Assembly of Vancouver indicated (see 2.3.2.4.). Yet this communion in faith required for the conciliar process is presupposed as already given, lived, and celebrated also in worship. It is not perceived as *a task still to be met,* for which reason the unity of the church is not counted — not even in a preliminary and secondary way — as part of the aim that the conciliar process itself pursues and *strives* to achieve.

Thus it would be incorrect in the final analysis to view the conciliar process, for all its importance, as a "model of ecclesiastical union" or as an effective development of the "federal-cooperative" model, despite great similarities.

"Rejection of the Inward Orientation" of the Ecumenical Movement

It is not an outsider's judgment of the conciliar process that it does not represent a model of ecclesiastical union. Rather, it is its explicitly and implicitly expressed self-understanding.

It is said again and again in one way or another that in the conciliar process the ecumenical movement pushes out beyond the inner-ecclesiastical orientation into which it has moved and thus regains its original orientation to the "whole oikumene of God." Konrad Raiser, General Secretary of the World Council of Churches since 1993, is quoted here as a representative of this view.[195] He recently reiterated what he has said in similar fashion many times since the World Council Assembly in Vancouver and in part has explained in detail and in historic perspective.[196]

> What moves the ecumenical movement? The reference remains important, indeed, that the challenge still very much exists to make the unity of the church that God wills visible; yet the reference also falls short. . . . The central problem areas of the discussion on unity in church and theology, that is, the questions of offices, the binding authority in doctrine, and the common structures of decision-making, are, for the majority of church members, problems internal to church institutions, problems that have little or nothing at all to do with their experience of reality.
>
> It is in the context of the Conciliar Process for Justice, Peace, and the Integrity of Creation and its great assemblies that the wider profile of the ecumenical movement once again broke forth. For in this process, the focus was not the church in the first instance but rather life in the world, the whole oikumene of God. At the center stood the effort for the common witness of Christian hope in view of the threats to life.
>
> (The ecumenical movement) cannot be restricted to the question of interchurch communion. The horizon of this movement is God's whole oikumene, the hope for a "new heaven and a new earth where justice dwells." The ecumenical movement may be understood as today's form of the pilgrim people of God with their eyes fixed on the goal which is shalom for all of creation, that is, wholeness, peace, justice, reconciliation in the presence of God. . . . And thus the aim of "visible unity in one faith and one eucharistic communion" is also only an interim aim.[197]

195. Konrad Raiser, "Modelle kirchlicher Einheit. Die Debatte der siebziger Jahre und die Folgerungen für heute," in *ÖR* (1987): 213.

196. For instance, in his article "Modelle kirchlicher Einheit" (see footnote 195 above), 195ff., esp. 210-15. It is developed in greatest detail and in an extensive ecumenical-historical and theological perspective in his book, *Ecumenism in Transition: A Paradigm Shift in the Ecumenical Movement* (Geneva: World Council of Churches, 1991), esp. chs. 4 and 5.

197. "Was bewegt die ökumenische Bewegung?" in *600 Jahre Kloster Frenswege* (1994), 14f.

What is said here about the rejection by the ecumenical movement of the church's "internal problems," about the world as the "whole oikumene of God," and about the visible unity of the church as merely an "interim aim" of the ecumenical movement is reflected again in the large conciliar assemblies in Basel and Seoul and in their final documents. The visible unity of the churches in faith as an ecumenical problem and aim of the ecumenical effort has to a large extent been set aside.[198] If, as had been stated, the visible unity of the churches has been granted the rank of an "interim aim," it is, nonetheless, clear that the conciliar process itself is not dedicated to this "interim aim." It has in view another aim that can be separated from that "interim aim."

The aim of the conciliar process is, indeed, fundamentally separable from the declared aim of the ecumenical movement. This can neither be doubted, nor can the conciliar process be reproached for representing this separability. For the mutual commitment of the churches and Christians for justice, peace, and the integrity of creation, a measure of agreement in faith is, in fact, sufficient that would be insufficient for the overcoming of interecclesiastical divisions and for the communion of the churches among one another.

This can be seen easily from what is stated in the third part of the final document from Basel about "Our Common Faith."[199] It is essentially a confession of the Triune God, who desires justice and grants peace and reconciliation, a confession of God, the creator of the world and human beings, whose love of creation remains steadfast even if human beings reject his will and his love. It is also a confession of the church, the body of Christ, and the people of God, whom God elects and calls so that they testify to his love and grace in the world.

Such a common faith can in fact be the "foundation of our responsibility"[200] and bear the "conciliar process of mutual commit-

198. The absence of the question of ecclesiastical unity in the final document of Seoul is completely obvious. In the document from Basel this is not true to the same degree. The problem of division and unity of the churches is at least mentioned there, e.g., nos. 39, 40, 43, 45 (p. 63), 48, 65.

199. Basel Final Document, nos. 21–40. European Ecumenical Assembly, *Frieden in Gerechigkeit.*

200. Thus the title of chapter III of the Basel Final Document. European Ecumenical Assembly, *Frieden in Gerechtigkeit.*

ment for justice, peace, and the integrity of creation." But such a common faith cannot yet be a basis for that communion of churches in faith which the ecumenical movement seeks and for which it struggles.

The assembly at Basel itself says that very clearly. It states that, in spite of that "common content of our faith," the "confessions are divided";[201] it recognizes that by baptism and faith we Christians are already in Christ but still do not live in full communion.[202] It is aware that that common content of the faith does not abolish the division at the Lord's table.[203]

It so happens that communion among the churches requires a considerably larger measure and greater density of common faith than the communion of the churches demands in its social-ethical responsibility toward the world. This difference is legitimate and should be recognized and not obscured.

For then the conciliar process presents itself for what it is, as an expression of the responsibility, arising from faith and borne by common convictions of faith, that all churches and Christians bear in face of today's threats to human existence, a responsibility borne irrespective of any divisions still existing in the church's faith. And then the ecumenical effort also remains what it is and always was: the struggle of churches and Christians for a communion in faith that regains the unity that was sundered among them.

The Relation between the Conciliar Process and Efforts of Ecclesiastical Unity

Could and should not both efforts, growing from faith with their different concepts of the aim, together have their equally essential place in the ecumenical movement?

This could be the case. Yet a mere juxtaposition of the two efforts or movements would conflict with the understanding of the

201. Basel Final Document, no. 21. European Ecumenical Assembly, *Frieden in Gerechtigkeit.*

202. Basel Final Document, no. 39. European Ecumenical Assembly, *Frieden in Gerechtigkeit.*

203. Basel Final Document, no. 40. European Ecumenical Assembly, *Frieden in Gerechtigkeit.*

unity of the church and thus also with the self-understanding of the ecumenical movement. For the dimension of common mission, of common witness and service in the world and for the world (see above 2.3.2.3.; cf. 2.3.1.) belongs indissolubly to the understanding of the unity of the church that shapes and informs the ecumenical movement. This is a matter of the integrity of the ecumenical movement.

To this extent, it is correct that the conciliar process understands itself as "ecumenical." It is not just "ecumenical" because all, or at least many and different, churches take part in it. It is also not "ecumenical" because one wishes to understand under "oikumene" the "entire world of God." Rather the conciliar process is "ecumenical" because its concern — stated briefly, the common responsibility for the world of all churches and Christians — belongs indissolubly to the understanding of the visible unity of the church and thus to the integrity of the "ecumenical" movement aiming at the visible unity of the church.

This means, however, that the conciliar process itself, in claiming to be ecumenical, may not depart from the comprehensive ecumenical movement and its aim.

Yet exactly this occurs the moment when the conciliar process perceives the aim of visible unity of the church "only as an interim aim" that does not concern it. This happens also wherever the process understands its specific, legitimate, and necessary concern as more important, more relevant, and more a priority than perhaps the effort for the communion of the churches in faith, sacraments, and ministry. This happens all the more where those involved in the conciliar process demand a comprehensive "new orientation," a "shift in perspective,"[204] or a *"paradigm shift"*[205] of the ecumenical movement that one-sidedly focuses on the specific concern of the conciliar process and that no longer preserves the multidimensional aim and thus the fundamental continuity of the ecumenical movement.

The threat that arises then is not only that the integrity of the ecumenical movement might be lost but also that its essential indi-

204. Raiser, *Modelle kirchlicher Einheit,* 213. (See footnote 195.)

205. Raiser, *Ecumenism in Transition* (see footnote 196), and the general language of "old" and "new paradigm" of the ecumenical movement (cf. footnote 133 in ch. 2).

visibility is called into question. For this indivisibility stands or falls not least with the common determination of the aim (see 1.2.).

That the indivisibility and wholeness of the ecumenical movement can be subject to question was seen already at the WCC Assembly of Vancouver, where the Conciliar Process took its formal start. It was stated there:

> At this Assembly we have sensed a tension between some of those who are concerned with the unity of the Church and others concerned with the desperate need for justice, peace and reconciliation in the human community. For some, the search for a unity in one faith and one eucharistic fellowship seems, at best secondary, at worst irrelevant to the struggles for peace, justice and human dignity; for others the Church's political involvement against the evils of history seems, at best, secondary, at worst detrimental to its role as eucharistic community and witness to the Gospel.[206]

This tension appears to have increased rather than lessened in the period after the Assembly and the development of the conciliar process. Therefore, it was commendable that a conference of the WCC, meeting in Denmark in February 1993, asked more precise questions about "the interaction between the Conciliar Process . . . and the discussion on the unity (of the church)" and showed itself unwilling merely to adjure "the indivisibility of the efforts for unity and those for justice."[207] One has to admit, nevertheless, that even here the mediation between the two "efforts" did not succeed and remains problematic. For the concept of "koinonia" that was to achieve mediation[208] appears once again to divide itself into two very different understandings of koinonia that are not really bridged and related to each other through a clear coordination.[209]

206. Vancouver (see footnote 192), 49.

207. Report of the meeting edited by Thomas F. Best and Wesley Granberg-Michaelson, *Koinonia and Justice, Peace, and Creation: Costly Unity: Presentations and Reports from the World Council of Churches' Consultation in Ronde, Denmark, February 1993* (Geneva: World Council of Churches, 1993), nos. 1 and 2.

208. Best and Granberg-Michaelson, *Costly Unity,* nos. 11–24.

209. On the one hand, it is said that "involvement in these struggles of human community generates this koinonia," so that common ethical action is "ecclesiogenetic" and constitutive of koinonia (no. 5, cf. no. 6). On the other hand, it is said:

In summing up one must say that the conciliar process, in the form in which it has been described and developed since 1983, does not understand itself as a model of ecclesiastical union. At the same time, it raises questions which not only touch the search for *models* of ecclesiastical union but, beyond that, the basic *understanding of church unity* and with it the aim of the ecumenical movement. The debate caused by this is far more important for the ecumenical movement than that of the 1970s. Its outcome is still open. Everything depends on whether the conciliar process finds an orientation in the future that more clearly integrates it into the framework of the ecumenical movement's current determination of its aim.

"The church is not *constituted* by or dependent for its ongoing existence upon the moral activities of its members. Its origin and on-going life rests in the lavish grace and patience of God" (no. 7.2). The correlation of a primarily "ethical" and a primarily "theological" understanding of koinonia finally remains unclear. The World Conference for Faith and Order in Santiago de Compostela (1993) also seems not to have gone further on this important point.

4. Assessment and Perspectives

"Crisis of the Ecumenical Movement"?

This volume began by citing the importance of the question of the concept of the ecumenical aim. As "a goal-oriented movement," the ecumenical movement "must articulate as clearly as possible the aims commonly agreed upon by its adherents. Both clarity and common agreement of the aim are indispensable. For diffuse concepts of the aim deprive the ecumenical movement of its orientation and paralyze its dynamics. Divergent concepts of the aim endanger its cohesion, its inner unity and indivisibility, and would bring the movement into self-contradiction." (See 1.1.)

The present situation of the ecumenical movement shows in an alarming manner the accurateness of this statement.

This volume appears at a point when the "crisis of the ecumenical movement" has been discussed already for a long time. Certainly, that is a very sweeping statement that must and can be countered. A historical retrospect also shows that this reference has accompanied the ecumenical movement like a shadow.

There are many reasons and indications, however, that prevent us from downplaying things. The signs of a deterioration of the ecumenical urgency are immense. There is a palpable decrease of common interest in ecumenical themes, events, and publications. The underlying loss in ecumenical motivation is connected with a disdain for the ecumenical achievement and an uncertainty of ecumenical orientation. Reservation and resistance, with which the ecumenical movement had always to struggle, gain new power.

Uncertainty in the Determination of Ecumenicity

A detailed position paper of the Institute for Ecumenical Research in Strasbourg, entitled *Crisis and Challenge of the Ecumenical Movement: Integrity and Indivisibility,* has recently sought to analyze the causes and characteristics of this "crisis." It agrees with the observation of others that the "uncertainty or . . . conflict . . . *in view of the ecumenical goal* and the methods to reach this goal" is one of the important characteristics of the present crisis.[1] The Strasbourg position paper demonstrated this in its analysis of the present ecumenical situation regarding various points, in particular the following:

- There is a common tendency to be content with the present ecumenical achievement and to leave matters as they are with the present existing peaceful and cooperative coexistence of the churches. This represents, however, a *downgrading of the ecumenical aim,* which is nothing less than the "fully committed fellowship" (koinonia) of the churches (see 2.3.2.4.).[2]
- The ecclesiastical reception of the doctrinal consensus worked out in the interconfessional dialogues turned out to be more difficult than expected and in many cases seems not to materialize. The resulting disappointments are often evident in the call for abandoning doctrinal consensus and efforts at achieving it among churches — the "end of consensus ecumenism." This goes hand in hand with the view that currently existing contrasts in the understanding of the apostolic faith, in the interpretation and use of the sacraments, and in the conception and practice of ecclesial offices can be left as they are (cf. above 3.3.3.).[3] But this *empties the ecumenical aim of its content.* For the sought-after, visible unity of the churches must become "visible"

1. *Crisis and Challenge of the Ecumenical Movement: Integrity and Indivisibility* (Geneva: WCC Publications, 1994), here no. 63.
2. *Crisis and Challenge,* nos. 14–16.
3. *Crisis and Challenge,* nos. 27–29.

and be experienced in a clear, reliable agreement in the confession of faith, in the sacraments, and in ministry that is capable of being articulated. Here lies one of the constitutive and indispensable elements of the church's unity (cf. above 2.3.1.).

- The present uncertainty regarding the ecumenical aim is demonstrated especially in a widespread tendency that the Strasbourg position paper characterizes and describes as "polarization of life and work," of "struggle for communion in faith," on the one hand, and "struggle for communion in life and action," on the other.[4] It is a tendency whose polarizing impulses proceed most clearly and in part even violently from a one-sided stress on action directed toward the world — from the unity of the churches *ad extra* — and which disregard the effort for unity of the church *ad intra,* for its visible unity in the confession of faith, in the sacraments, and in the ecclesiastical office (ministry). The result of this is a *disintegration and reduction of the determination of the ecumenical aim* with regard to the different dimensions and aspects of visible unity that belong together (cf. 2.3.1.).

Such a tendency to disintegration and reduction of the multidimensionality of ecclesiastical unity was repeatedly encountered in the course of the preceding presentation, for instance, in the stress on the mission of the church (see 2.3.2.3.), in the conciliar process (see 3.3.4.), as well as in the more distant history of the ecumenical movement with its cooperative-federal basic model of ecclesiastical union (see 3.2.1.). We have seen how the declared aim of the ecumenical movement is questioned there not only implicitly but also explicitly, and how one can call for a radical "new orientation" or a "paradigm shift" of the ecumenical movement (see 2.3.2.3.).

Integrity and Indivisibility of the Ecumenical Movement

Questioning the ecumenical aim in such a way affects the ecumenical movement as a whole.

Is it really the case that the aim of the ecumenical movement is the visible unity of the church, as it is especially determined in the

4. *Crisis and Challenge,* nos. 34–38 and 63.

New Delhi declaration of unity and its subsequent development up to the Assembly in Canberra, and that this is where the *integrity* of the movement truly resides?

And given all the diversity in legitimate emphases within this determination of aim and all the variations in the trends and manifestations of the ecumenical movement, is it possible still to see in it a single movement that, in the final analysis, is held together by a commonly understood aim and thus preserves its *indivisibility* on which it stands or falls as a "movement of unity"?

This book pleads for a decisive affirmative answer to both questions. In this respect, it is not written *sine ira et studio*. This plea, however, appears in this book mainly as a descriptive account chiefly concerned with tracing how the aim to which the ecumenical movement strives and by which it is oriented has been ever more clearly understood and described.

The first decades of the ecumenical movement were marked by unconnected and divergent simultaneity of differently directed movements and the failure to include all confessional groups of Christendom and their specific concepts of unity. This presentation has shown how these initial decades were followed by comprehensive steps toward integration that can be referenced by three key events: the two assemblies of the World Council of Churches in Amsterdam (1948) and in New Delhi (1961) and Vatican II with its decree on ecumenism (1964).

It was decisive that these initially only external integrations also found expression in a determination of the ecumenical aim in a hitherto unmatched clarity and integrative strength, namely, the New Delhi declaration of unity (cf. above 2.3.1.). That declaration became the Magna Carta of ecumenism, capable of warranting that integration on the basis of the ecumenical effort's interior point of reference and orientation (i.e., the common understanding of church unity) and thereby giving the ecumenical movement its inner integrity and indivisibility.

The time of vacillation about the aim of the ecumenical movement was now over in principle, as was the time of its divisibility into movements and "ecumenisms" that were unrelated one to another and becoming independent.

This certainly did not mean that all the traces of that uncertainty in the determination of the ecumenical aim were now erased.

The debate of the 1970s about the models of ecclesiastical union demonstrates that. It shows at the same time, however, that the conflicts between the different models of union can be overcome in light of the common understanding of the unity of the church (see above 3.3.1., especially 3.3.1.4.).

Nor did it mean that no problems any longer existed with determining the aim of ecumenicity. From the legitimate emphasis on the churches' common mission and their common action in the world, tendencies developed that questioned the hitherto existing determination of the aim and sought to give a new and different orientation to ecumenicity (cf. above 2.3.2.3. and 3.3.4.). Yet in light of the comprehensive and multidimensional understanding of unity that informs the ecumenical movement, these tendencies lack foundation because the concerns behind these tendencies have their full and undiminished place in that understanding of unity itself.

Finally, it did not mean that that determination of the aim was so fixed that it was not capable or even in need of further explication and development. Quite to the contrary, it became apparent (see above 2.3.2.) that such further explications and developments took place very soon and extend even to the present, though the basic continuity of the ecumenical aim has been preserved. It may be assumed that more such developments will take place in the future. For not only will new ecumenical experiences and insights necessarily bring them about but also changing circumstances in the life of Christians and churches where they are called to make their oneness visible.

Precisely the multidimensionality of the understanding of church unity prevents the ecumenical effort *in concreto* from dedicating itself to all dimensions and aspects of unity at the same time and in the same way. The more ecumenical effort is active and alive the more it will address different concrete possibilities and demands, situations and interests. This is not only legitimate but also necessary.

What is decisive, however, for the integrity and indivisibility of the ecumenical movement is that these accentuations recognize themselves as such and in this sense relativize their own claims. The criterion to which they must be subjected is whether they let themselves be integrated into the multidimensional understanding of the church's unity that the ecumenical movement takes as its aim, or whether they isolate themselves from it and then are virtually forced to present themselves wrongly as the whole and real aim of ecumenicity.

The "Correlation" of the Dimensions of Ecclesiastical Unity

Yet in view of the present tendencies toward an erosion, disintegration, or reduction of the determination of the ecumenical aim, it is hardly sufficient only to refer to the "sense of belonging together" of the different aspects and dimensions of visible unity. Certainly, the affirmation of their fundamental affinity and togetherness already achieves a great deal. Such an additive view, however, remains unsatisfactory and is threatened by disintegration and reduction.

Therefore, it is far more than a question of style when the ecumenical declarations of unity — and the New Delhi declaration is exemplary here — do not simply enumerate and tally the individual aspects and constitutive elements of visible unity but rather link them together, relate them one to another, and bind them in a holistic view, in brief, "integrate them."

If we want to speak correctly about the aim of the ecumenical movement, then it is absolutely essential to note and consider this *"correlation"* of the individual aspects and dimensions of the visible unity of the church. It is not arbitrary and reversible as the sequence of a numerical column is in relation to the final sum. The correlation is not only logical. It is theological.

Once more and for the last time, we refer to the New Delhi declaration of unity (see above 2.3.1.), which is succeeded by others and to which they correspond:

The arc of these statements about the visible unity of the church as a "fully committed fellowship" leads from common baptism and the common confession of Christ to the common faith, confession, and proclamation of the apostolic message of salvation, on to communion in the Lord's Supper, to common prayer and common life, up to common service to others and common action directed toward the world.

This arc may not be split up into its parts or cut off at any one place. It also must not be reversed in its total direction. It is integrated and irreversible and corresponds in this to the biblical understanding of unity or communion of the faithful. The present reflection on the New Testament/early church concept of koinonia/communio in its integrative power (see 2.3.2.4.) should help in recognizing this clearly.